Teacher-Led
Development
Work

Teacher-Led Development Work

Guidance and Support

David Frost and Judy Durrant

David Fulton Publishers
London

David Fulton Publishers Ltd
The Chiswick Centre, 414 Chiswick High Road, London W4 5TF

www.fultonpublishers.co.uk

First published in Great Britain 2003 by David Fulton Publishers

British Library Cataloguing in Publication Data
A catalogue record for this book is available from the British Library.

ISBN 1 84312 006 2

Typeset in Great Britain by Keyset Composition, Colchester, Essex
Printed and bound in Great Britain

Contents

Foreword by John MacBeath   vii

Other perspectives   ix

About this book   xi

Part A   A theory of teacher leadership   1

Part B   Establishing partnerships and networks to support
             teacher-led development work   7

Part C   A framework for teacher-led development work   23

Part D   Leading development work in schools: a guide for teachers   27

Part E   Supporting development work in schools: a guide for
             external support   51

Part F   Workshops   69

Part G   Resources   93

References   139

Index   143

Foreword by John MacBeath

Teachers as leaders? It is a challenging notion at a time when teachers are reporting new levels of stress, disenchantment and 'deprofessionalisation' (Price Waterhouse Cooper 2001; Johnson and Hallgarten 2002; Galton and MacBeath 2002). What room is there for teacher leadership in a policy climate in which government dictates and teachers follow? A climate in which policy makers talk in terms of 'delivery', casting teachers in the role of ambassadors of government to the world of children. Teachers are struggling to come to terms with demands for accountability – not to the needs of children themselves or their parents, but to government departments and inspectors.

David Frost and Judy Durrant are optimists, possibly incurable, a condition brought about by their constant contact with teachers and classrooms on a week-by-week basis. They are acutely aware of the expectations and pressures that constrain the teaching task but they also observe how creative teachers can work in the spaces. They understand the paradoxes of school and classroom life – creative discontent, orderly chaos, confident uncertainty. They witness regularly how frustration can be turned into excitement and the infectious quality of that, not just within one classroom but across a whole school, beyond into local school clusters, and even across national borders. In the so-called 'information age', it is a startling insight that imaginative practice in one classroom can travel the world.

Good ideas and innovative practice do not, however, spread of their own accord; they require support, frameworks and critical friendship. They are embedded in principles of 'knowledge creation and transfer', inherently sceptical of simplistic notions of 'transmission'. Herein is the genius of this volume – a strong underpinning respect for good theory married to pragmatics and devilish detail. It is in the injunction to get the workshop setting right, to attend to the small things: the recalcitrant technology, the heating that the caretaker may have programmed to switch off at four o' clock, the glass of wine as more than a symbolic accoutrement.

Themes run through the book as continuous threads – telling your story, sharing, challenging, generating professional knowledge, increasing the stock of understanding and expertise. Discovering the treasures within the everyday, making the invisible visible, rendering the implicit explicit, taking the initiative, practising leadership by doing it; these are messages that are returned to persistently and are embedded in the cornucopia of exemplars and resources. The authors wish to dispel the myth that educational literature contains only 'theory'. In these pages the medium *is* the message. Theory in practice. There is nothing so practical as a good theory.

Dispelling myths is an important prelude to the many and varied activities contained in this book. This is sometimes described as 'reframing' or 'borderless thinking'. It challenges inert ideas. Leadership is exercised not simply at the apex of the organisation. Professional development is not an event. Improvement is not mandated by government. Good practice is not disseminated by the dead hand of bureaucracy.

And this is not a book – at least not in the sense of a good bedtime read. It is a guide on the side. It is like a Michelin travelogue that you peruse, flick the pages and alight on somewhere you have always wanted to go. The authors use words such as 'reconnaissance', 'the terrain', 'exploring', implying that teacher leadership is a journey, whose starting point is anticipation and adventure and its goal a new and wonderful place to be.

> John MacBeath is Professor of Educational Leadership at the
> University of Cambridge Faculty of Education.

Other perspectives

Lesley Saunders

This is a deceptive book: written in a tactful, meticulous and rather modest way, it is none the less quite radical in the propositions it sets out for teachers' professionalism and professional development and in the very proper presumptions it makes about the need for, and desirability of, teacher-led school improvement.

It is also very timely – there is undoubtedly a sense abroad amongst many policy-makers, practitioners and scholars alike that, without the engagement of the hearts and minds of teachers acting as leaders and agents of change, further educational reform will be stymied, and probably not even viable.

The authors say (on p. 13) that 'real improvement stems from participation in a discourse that is both critical and authentic'. If we add to that 'and is also creative and energising' then we have a very good idea about the tone and significance of this book. It is firmly rooted in the daily practice of the classroom and also in the best tradition of scholarly approaches to reflection and evaluation – but its branches spread out into the bright open air of the ideals and vision that attract most teachers to teaching in the first place.

Lesley Saunders was formerly Head of School Improvement Centre at the National Foundation for Educational Research, and is currently Policy Adviser for Research at the General Teaching Council for England.

Graham Handscomb

This is a book of great value. It has the potential to become a seminal guide for teachers wanting to reclaim their sense of professionalism and to genuinely lead development in their own classrooms and schools. The book's particular strength is that it starts from the premise that teachers' lives will continue to be pressurised and that schools will remain complex change environments. With reference to recent research, the authors acknowledge squarely that ten years of 'top-down' reform has led to intolerable workloads and has inhibited teachers' capacity to initiate and sustain their own development activity. By providing this grounded and systematic manual, they seek to change all that.

The great merit of the book is that this practical set of development tools is thoroughly founded on carefully established theory of teacher development, drawing on key literature and the authors' own research and wide practice in schools. The net result is to inspire confidence and credibility in the approaches advocated and, most importantly, to inspire teachers and to convince them that development work is not only do-able but that it can significantly help to transform the quality of their worklife.

Graham Handscomb is Head of Best Practice and Research, Essex Local Education Authority.

Gary Holden

Over a six-year period in a Kent comprehensive school, my colleagues and I employed the methods and principles described in this inspiring book. For me, this volume sums up with passion, clarity and humanity the values, processes and outcomes of teacher-led development work.

I worked alongside teachers who followed the process described here and saw at first hand how they were enabled to take control of their own professional lives and to play a real and tangible role in school improvement. As a senior manager I saw these teachers become central figures in building the school's capacity to initiate, sustain and build on change.

David Frost and Judy Durrant provide us with an invaluable map of the values, principles and processes that underpin teacher-led development work, a map that unites practitioners, schools, districts and universities working in partnership towards a single destination: the creation of learning communities in our schools.

Gary Holden was formerly acting Deputy Head at St John's RC Comprehensive School, Gravesend, Kent, and is currently Deputy Head at Borden Grammar School, Sittingbourne, Kent.

Jane McGregor

This book acknowledges and celebrates the complexity of contexts for teacher-led development work. It engages with the web of relationships that comprise the school, within and beyond the institution, paying close attention to the type of interactions that create and sustain meaningful change and improvements in teaching and learning. A particular strength of the book is the authentic and practical support it provides, evolving from grounded experience, as a starting point for individuals, groups of teachers and wider networks involved in school-based development and enquiry. In emphasising the importance and realities of teachers' strategic leadership of such development, it addresses the form of collaborative and collegial relationships that are frequently invoked but rarely mapped out. The elegant but robust combination of theory and practice provides a framework that will be of use to teachers and those involved in arrangements to support teacher leadership. In providing practical suggestions for this support, the book makes a real contribution to the evolution of the dynamic and reflective communities of practice which can transform the teaching and learning relationships in our schools.

Jane McGregor was formerly specialist adviser to the TTA teacher research panel and is a member of the Networked Learning Communities programme team.

About this book

What is it for?

This book presents and explains an approach to school improvement that rests on the belief that it is teachers who are at the 'sharp edge' of processes of development and improvement (Bascia and Hargreaves 2000). Effectiveness in teaching and learning inevitably depends on their imagination, creativity, effort and commitment. It depends on their capacity to exercise leadership to bring about change. The approach to school improvement presented here integrates a number of elements that support teachers' leadership and professional action. This capacity is nurtured by management structures and professional cultures within schools, but these are developed most effectively and fully when teachers play an active part in their development. The capacity of teachers to make a difference is made more powerful through links between schools committed to learning together. It is also strengthened by the inclusion of an external dimension to the support as schools form partnerships and collaborative arrangements with other institutions and agencies. This approach is intended to contribute to the 'reprofessionalisation' of teachers, reinstating them as the key agents of educational change and improvement.

Who is it for?

The book provides practical guidance both for teachers who wish to initiate and sustain development work in their schools and for those who may want to provide a framework of support for those teachers. Specifically, it provides guidance for:

- teachers and others leading development work;
- head teachers/principals/senior managers promoting and supporting inclusive leadership;
- coordinators, facilitators, mentors, consultants, advisers and university staff supporting teachers' development work;
- organisations and agencies providing and coordinating schemes and networks that support teachers' leadership.

While the book has been written specifically with teachers and schools in mind, the framework can also be used within other organisations and professional contexts where practitioners want to lead change in their own professional situations.

What does it do?

The book sets out a systematic process, developed and refined over a ten-year period, through which teachers can lead development work in their own schools. It helps them to pursue initiatives arising from their own professional concerns and responsibilities within the context of school development priorities. The complexity of school change is acknowledged and leadership issues are addressed. Collaborative working, the use of evidence, action planning and review are emphasised to ensure that the work has maximum impact. Critical reflection and evaluation are central to the process so that both personal professional development and the school's organisational learning are enhanced. We offer this approach as a strategy for enabling teachers not only to make more of a difference in their own schools, but also, through networking and participation in a wider professional discourse, to contribute to the development of professional knowledge as a whole.

Following a rationale for this approach, the guidance is presented in the form of brief explanations, checklists and other practical materials. Formats, facsimiles, vignettes and case studies are provided to help teachers plan and document their development work.

How is it organised?

There are seven parts to this book:

Part A   A theory of teacher leadership
This section provides a brief overview of the theory which underpins this approach to school improvement and sets out a rationale for the particular focus on teacher-led development work.

Part B   Establishing partnerships and networks to support teacher-led development work
Part B contains guidance for school leaders and external agencies on the establishment and operation of school-based and school-focused partnerships, initiatives and networks designed to support teacher-led development work and school improvement. This includes examples of a number of projects illustrating applications of this approach in different contexts.

Part C   A framework for teacher-led development work
This part presents and explains a framework to guide teachers' planning, leadership and evaluation of development work. It provides a rationale and structure for the practical guidance in subsequent sections.

Part D   Leading development work in schools: a guide for teachers
This section contains detailed guidance to support individual teachers through the stages of leading development work in their own professional situations. It includes materials to support the planning of development work and evaluation to maximise impact.

Part E   Supporting development work in schools: a guide for external support
This provides detailed guidance for those supporting teachers' leadership including facilitators, tutors and mentors. Practical issues and professional dilemmas in supporting teachers as leaders are discussed. Guidance is given on providing academic supervision in the context of award-bearing programmes.

Part F   Workshops

This section presents a series of workshops and activities that can be used with groups to support different elements and aspects of the process of teacher-led development work.

Part G   Resources

The final part contains a range of resources such as formats for planning documents, briefings and discussion papers, examples and facsimiles, checklists and review guides. These materials can be photocopied for use within support groups or by individuals.

We hope that colleagues will find the ideas and materials in this book useful, but we expect that users will want to develop them further to suit their own contexts. We would be very interested to hear from anyone who has been able to do this so that we can continue to develop the approach and learn from a wide range of experience.

David Frost and Judy Durrant
dcf20@cam.ac.uk
jd24s@cant.ac.uk

Part A

A theory of teacher leadership

In this book we focus on how teachers can take the lead in improving the quality and effectiveness of teaching and learning. We believe that this is a neglected perspective in the study of school effectiveness and the pursuit of school improvement.

Teacher leadership and capacity building

Whether the impetus for change springs from national reforms or from the perception of a single teacher that something could be better, improvements in teaching and learning ultimately depend on the action taken by teachers. Of course with 'top-down' initiatives, the compliance of teachers can be secured – as recent UK numeracy and literacy strategies have demonstrated – but real and lasting improvement depends on individual teachers' commitment and enthusiasm for improvement and this cannot simply be dictated from above. So, we are centrally concerned here with the capacity of individual teachers, with or without formal management responsibility, to exercise leadership and take greater responsibility for the development and improvement of professional practice.

This is not to argue for a return to some kind of mythical golden age of teacher autonomy. On the contrary, our view is based on the clear understanding that teachers are members of teams and organisations dedicated to public service, and so are properly accountable to a range of stake-holders. However, the organisational capacity of schools depends on the personal and interpersonal capacity of teachers (Mitchell and Sackney 2000), that is, the extent to which they can develop their professional knowledge and skill, and form and sustain collaborative relationships with their colleagues. It is through collaboration that schools can develop the coherence of values and the consistency of practice that characterise effectiveness (Sammons *et al.* 1995).

The organisational conditions in schools are not simply created by head teachers or principals, rather they are the product of interactive processes. Theories that assume a hierarchical model of organisation suggest that these conditions are the result of the resolution of 'top-down' and 'bottom-up' power. The assumption within this view of organisations is that head teachers and others with management responsibility (now often called 'the leadership team') take strategic action and teachers respond by exercising 'bottom-up' power. On the one hand the response may be compliance, perhaps because there is a high level of trust between the teachers and their managers or because there happens to be a very high level of consensus within the school. On the other hand, teachers may resist change by passive inertia or perhaps by articulating and voicing their opposition to practices introduced precipitously by those in formal leadership positions.

Teachers may not recognise these responses as the exercise of power, but head teachers and principals who have attempted to lead their schools through a process of change and improvement are likely to be in no doubt that members of their staff exercise power. They know that both pedagogical practice and the organisational conditions in the school are shaped by factors associated with the school's culture. We take the term *culture* in this context to mean the complex patterns of habitual behaviour, expectations, the entrenched beliefs and values of teachers, expressed through the power relations that result from the school's particular history (Hargreaves 1995). Head teachers and principals also know that the process of micro-political negotiation is very hard to manage and can result in a level of organisational chaos that is unproductive and damaging to the school's effectiveness. From the point of view of the head teacher or principal, it may be tempting to embrace an authoritarian model of leadership in the attempt to promote effectiveness. This may involve adopting draconian measures to try to establish particular structures or practices. Such approaches may well show short-term gains, but research suggests that long-term and sustained improvement depends on what is often referred to as 'capacity building' (Gray *et al.* 1999). Capacity building is a term used increasingly in the school improvement literature to refer to the school's capacity to improve itself. John MacBeath's work tends to rely on Stoll's generic definition: 'Internal capacity is the power to engage in and sustain continuous learning of teachers and the school itself for the purpose of enhancing pupil learning' (Stoll *et al.* 2001: 171). We find this definition helpful but, like Mitchell and Sackney (2000), want to extend it to include collegial decision-making, which is essential for a school that aspires to be a learning community.

Shared vision

The key to capacity building is the concept of teacher leadership which has the potential to help us avoid the limitations of the hierarchical model of school organisation. Teacher leadership is about the cultivation and use of power, but the term 'bottom-up' is not appropriate. It is more a matter of teachers being able to exercise leadership within a coherent collegial framework; but what do we assume leadership to be? For us there are three key words: *values*, *vision* and *strategy*. Our assumption is that the process of leadership begins with the clarification of values and the articulation of a vision underpinned by those values. Vision we take to be the result of imagining what could be and what ought to be. In addition, the exercise of leadership necessarily entails strategic action intended to realise those values in practice and narrow the gap between that vision and the current reality of professional practice. It might be suggested, of course, that an organisation in which so many people are promoting their own vision and acting strategically would be impossibly chaotic. However, comfort can be drawn from Fullan's arguments about complexity and moral purpose (Fullan 1999); he draws on Stacey's work (1996a, 1996b) to support the view that schools are inevitably complex and that we have no choice but to work to foster the sort of human interaction that leads to the growth of empathy and the pursuit of mutual interest. In this book, we offer strategies that help schools to resolve the tension between the personal vision building of individual teachers and the priorities of the school as an organisation.

We argue therefore that head teachers and principals need to adopt a model of leadership that facilitates such capacity building: so-called 'transformational leadership' (Leithwood and Jantzi 1990). Some have expressed misgivings about this: Mitchell and Sackney (2000) for example have suggested that transformational leadership is still just about the exercise of power at the apex of the organisation where the concern is to engage members of staff in the decision-making process as a means to 'get them on board'. For them, the problem remains that power is not distributed equitably. We take a slightly more realistic view which recognises that inevitably head teachers and principals have more of a grip on the levers of power. In support of this, Angus has argued:

> Those who hold administrative positions need to realise that their best contribution to educational reform may be to use the authority of their position to facilitate the exercise of agency of those of their staff who, for one reason or another, have begun to examine critically, and engage in dialogue about, educational issues and educational purposes so that they are rendered problematic and subjected to scrutiny (Angus 1993: 86).

Angus's argument rests on a theory about leadership that is not based on the structuralist tradition in which leadership styles are underpinned by values such as control, predictability and efficiency, but one which draws on Giddens's (1984) sociology to support the argument that teachers can play a significant part in shaping the 'conditions, structures, organizations, rules and agreements that shape their lives'.

We agree with the proposition that effective schools are those that have a high degree of coherence of values and consistency in practice (Sammons *et al.* 1995), but it is a question of how a shared vision is arrived at. Fullan (1993) promotes the view of Peter Senge who says that 'a shared vision is a vision that many people are truly committed to because it reflects their own personal values' (Senge 1990: 206). This is not to say that the school's development goals are to be based on some kind of amalgam of the personal values of its staff, but rather that they are fashioned and tempered through the kind of discourse within which values are clarified and examined.

Morale and agency

Arguably the national reforms of the past decade or so have achieved a great deal, but one of the costs has been the undermining of teacher morale. A discussion about morale is illuminated by the concept of human agency. Bruner argues that *agency* is a fundamental aspect of selfhood and that humankind is distinguished not simply by the capacity to initiate and sustain activity of its own volition, but most crucially by the capacity to construct a narrative: 'a record that is related to the past but that is also extrapolated into the future – self with history and with possibility' (Bruner 1996: 36). This capacity to 'narratise' necessarily involves moral choice about our actions and a sense of responsibility for them. Our actions require 'skill and know-how' and consequently involve self-evaluation which has a major impact on self-esteem. It is evident that teachers' sense of agency has been frustrated by the climate of 'performativity' that leads to a lowering of self-esteem. In this climate, teachers are judged by simplistic measures of students' academic performance, and so the opportunities for experiencing failure overwhelm the opportunities for experiencing success through the exercise of agency. The impact on the morale of teachers is evident in the prevailing difficulties with staff recruitment and retention. Recent research for Demos and the National Union of Teachers (Horne 2001) confirms that more than ten years of 'top-down' reform has led not only to intolerable workloads but, more fundamentally, to a demolition of a sense of agency. The massive increase in the use of counselling helplines (*Times Educational Supplement* (*TES*) 1999a) and claims made against local education authorities (LEAs) by teachers who have suffered stress-related breakdowns have been attributed variously to heavy workloads, external accountability and draconian management styles (*TES* 1999b, 2000; Webb and

Vulliamy 1996; Evans 1998). These therapeutic strategies may well be necessary at the present time, but in the long run they are not the answer. They are patronising and ineffective in tackling such a fundamental malaise. What we offer in this book instead is a strategy that addresses the question of teachers' sense of agency. In short, our approach offers practical support for teacher leadership.

The approach put forward here has been presented before in various stages of development (Frost 1995, 1997; Frost *et al.* 2000) and has been taken up enthusiastically although on a relatively small scale. However, in this early part of the new millennium, the climate is perhaps a little more auspicious. At the time of writing the policy discourse on school leadership is peppered with concepts such as 'shared leadership', 'distributed leadership', 'dispersed leadership' (Harris and Muijs 2002) and 'parallel leadership' (Crowther *et al.* 2002). The differences between these hinge on the question of whether teacher leadership is genuine leadership, if it is a commodity that can be distributed or shared by the head teacher or principal. Some writers avoid this conceptual problem by talking about 'leadership density' (Sergiovanni 2001) or a 'leader-rich culture' (Mitchell and Sackney 2000). Our own view is that, since head teachers and principals do have a disproportionate degree of power, they can choose to use it to create the conditions in which teacher leadership can flourish. Teachers also have power, but they may need practical support to enable them to deploy it more strategically and responsibly to ensure that their pupils' life chances are improved as a result.

Leadership for learning

Teacher leadership is often talked about in terms of the extent to which teachers can be persuaded to take on management roles, for example, subject leader or a short-term responsibility such as chair of a working party or school improvement group of some kind. Our view of teacher leadership is more inclusive in that we are addressing the need to encourage all teachers to be 'change agents' (Fullan 1993), whether or not they have such a formal role. Furthermore, we are interested in teachers' leadership of *development work* which implies an explicit focus on improvement and learning. For us, this highlights the need to focus on *leadership for learning* or *learner-centred leadership* (MacBeath forthcoming).

Development work has three essentially interrelated dimensions: (1) managing change through collaboration; (2) experimenting with practice; and (3) gathering and using evidence. There is a growing body of evidence to suggest that it is through such development work that teachers can make a major difference to the personal and interpersonal capacities of themselves and their colleagues, to pupils' learning, and to the organisational structures and cultures of their schools (Frost and Durrant 2002). In addition, they can make a significant contribution to wider professional discourse and professional knowledge creation and transfer.

However, our own research (Frost 1999; Frost 2000; Frost *et al.* 2000; Frost and Durrant 2002; Holden 2002a, 2002b) shows that teachers are unlikely to be able to engage in such leadership without a framework of support and expectations, at least not in large numbers. There has always been a minority of teachers with the ability and determination to take up this challenge. Often they have drawn support from participation in action research-based Masters degree programmes or an externally driven school improvement project. No doubt these projects have had some impact on practice (Elliott *et al.* 1996), but the numbers of teachers participating in such programmes are too small to make a major difference. Furthermore, the action research tradition has tended to become rather individualistic, neglecting the strategic dimension and featuring written accounts dominated by reflections on research methodology in dissertations for which the readership is limited to the university examiners.

Support for teacher leadership

So what is required to support teacher-led development work? We suggest that, first of all, head teachers and principals have to recognise and understand the potential for leadership in teachers. This is essential for two reasons. First, as we have argued above, head teachers and principals have both the power and the strategic position to create the internal structures and conditions that are conducive to teacher leadership. Second, head teachers and principals have the power to enable the school to enter into and build partnerships with other agencies to provide appropriate support for teachers' leadership of development work.

Partnerships with external agencies are important because they can bring to bear a range of different expertise and value orientations. External agents are also relatively untrammelled by the particular history and micro-politics of the school and can act as impartial critical friends. We argue here that university departments or faculties of education (UDEs) are particularly well placed to play a part in such partnerships because of their expertise in research, but just as important is their experience in providing structures to support teachers' reflection and presentation of accounts of their practice. This is not straightforward however, since the emphasis in some UDEs on their own research may well stand in the way of an orientation towards such work. Stenhouse's argument in the 1970s about the role of such bodies is more relevant than ever and one which has been echoed more recently by David Hargreaves (1998). Stenhouse (1975) was concerned with issues of authority and status, validation and accountability. He argued that members of UDEs should recognise that it is teachers who are best placed to understand classrooms and so the university staff should offer their skills in support of teachers' inquiry-based development work.

We are in no doubt that schools should engage with the values of higher education which includes putting a high premium on inquiry, evidence, scholarship and critical debate, but this is likely to be most effective when it takes place – in part at least – on the school site rather than solely within the cloistered world of the university. When teachers attend courses designed by university staff and held on the university campus, there is little sense of partnership. The partnership between schools and external agencies has to be a genuine one based on mutual respect for different values, missions, expertise and experience. It is important, therefore, that where schools control the funding, they should flex their muscles and negotiate a set of arrangements that fit their own agendas and make the best of local circumstances and the expertise and agendas of potential partners.

Once a partnership is established, it can provide a framework of support for teachers' leadership of development work. This can be done in the three major ways set out below.

- The provision of scaffolding for a process of reflection, planning and strategic action.
- The fostering of critical discourse through the provision of a support group and critical friendship.
- The extension of critical discourse through the development of a network.

Scaffolding for reflection, planning and strategic action

Some years ago, the term 'reflective action planning' was coined (Frost 1995) to try to suggest an explicit process of reflection, planning and strategic action through which teachers can exercise leadership in pursuit of development goals in which they have a stake. The process is represented in this book as a series of elements or stages such as *clarifying values and concerns* or *personal development planning*, each of which is explored through the use of workshops and scaffolding in the form of structures, formats, guidelines and examples.

Support for critical discourse

Teachers' development work can also be supported through participation in a discourse that is critical and authentic. Being critical is about making the familiar strange; stepping back from everyday concerns and subjecting them to scrutiny through inquiry, discussion and reflection. Being authentic is about focusing on concrete concerns rather than abstract generalities. Discussion and debate within a school-based support group enables teachers to examine the substantive themes and concerns central to their development work and to explore issues that arise from their leadership of that work. When such groups are cross-hierarchical and facilitated by external agencies, the discussion is freed up from the usual constraints and micro-political tensions (Ball 1987). Such discussions can provide mutual support and opportunities to reflect on roles and strategies.

The support can also work at the individual level through *critical friendship*, which we take to be help in the form of a dialogue with a trusted person who asks challenging questions and offers a different perspective and a constructive critique of the teacher's work (MacBeath 1998). Although it may be possible for LEA staff to play this role, we believe that university staff may have the advantage because they are free from the constraints of accountability and have experience of academic tutoring. Nevertheless, the scope of the dialogue needs to be extended beyond the usual academic concerns to encompass the strategic dimension.

Extending critical discourse through networking

A partnership can provide further support through establishing and maintaining a network. Contrast and collaboration are key tools for learning and so networking plays an important part in developing the critical perspective. Networking can be entirely local but a virtual dimension (web-based) enables the partnership to widen the parameters of the discourse and to link networks together. Networks enable teachers to share accounts of practice, but professional knowledge is not easily transformed through simple dissemination. Rather, we suggest that a network should be seen as a *community of practice* (Wenger 1998) in which teachers experience a sense of belonging. In such a community teachers share a set of values and purposes; contacts are made and relationships developed, and practice is explored and tested through evidence-based discussion and more active inter-school collaborative inquiry and evaluation. Such networks constitute vehicles through which teachers can not only make a real difference in their schools but also reach out to the wider professional community and contribute to national debate, policy formation and the development of professional knowledge as a whole.

The groups, networks and individual critical friendship organised within partnerships and supported by practical strategies and materials as described here provide firm foundations for teacher-led development work. We have seen that this approach can gradually and powerfully enhance individuals' agency and can be influential in building capacity within and between schools.

Part B

Establishing partnerships and networks to support teacher-led development work

This section provides guidance on the establishment and operation of partnerships and networks to support teachers in their leadership of development work. Here we explain how schools can work in partnership with each other, with universities, LEAs and other agencies to provide effective support.

As we argue in Part A, schools can build partnerships with each other and with these external agencies to negotiate arrangements that support teachers in exercising leadership to pursue development goals arising from their own concerns in the context of school, district and national agendas for change. Educational communities of academics, policy-makers and practitioners have a responsibility to work together to develop a climate in which professional knowledge is created and transformed. Teachers should have a central and active role in this process, which in practice means creating the right climate for teacher participation at the local and district level. We are therefore suggesting a model that goes far beyond the provision of various continuing professional development (CPD) activities, towards the creation of 'communities of practice' (Wenger 1998; McLaughlin 1997), fostering networks of critical discourse based on inquiry, evidence and experience, as well as comparison and contrast from a range of educational perspectives. Partnerships should be established to maximise the conditions supporting teacher involvement and mutual learning within these communities, so that all the partner organisations (not just the schools) are able to develop a better understanding of learning and teaching and the processes of school improvement in order to build powerful capacity for change.

This guidance material is organised as ten key strategies for partnership. At the end of this section a number of brief case studies illustrate a range of partnerships that have already been established.

The importance of partnership

We start with the assumption that if teachers are to exercise leadership in development work, they need support from participation in a programme or scheme based on a partnership between the school and external agencies. Teachers have always looked outside their school boundaries for help with their improvement and staff development agendas although this has not always been effective. We suggest that it is likely to be most effective when the school enters into a genuine partnership with other schools and with agencies such as universities and LEAs/school districts which have different kinds of expertise to offer. As we argued in Part A, these different institutions have their distinctive values, traditions and orientations that are both important and valuable, but in order to create the most effective form of support, they may need to adapt their practices. For example, in seeking to support teacher-led development work:

- *schools* may need to develop their organisational cultures in order to enable teachers to exercise leadership and to open up channels of communication that will allow teachers' initiatives to have an impact;

- *universities* may need to make adjustments to their accreditation frameworks and the way they conduct research, for example, academic staff will have to be prepared to work differently, visiting schools or professional development centres to provide tuition or lead seminars;

- *LEAs or school districts* may need to de-emphasise the accountability role of their advisory staff and develop instead their role in knowledge management which requires a non-judgemental perspective.

Within a scheme or programme to support teacher-led development work, arrangements, roles and relationships have to be tailored to the particular context, so there needs to be a thorough negotiation between potential partners that may lead to adjustments like those described above. They should be regularly reviewed and adapted over time as circumstances change (see Strategy 10 'Devise monitoring, evaluation and research strategies').

The values, purposes and intentions of the partners need to be clear to all those involved. It is important that they are discussed and agreed to avoid misunderstandings about the nature of the work. It may be useful to return to them as the progress of a particular project or initiative is reviewed.

We strongly suggest that the partners should draw up a contract, memorandum of agreement or other document which sets out as clearly as possible the expectations that each partner has of the other. A facsimile of such a document can be found in Resource 1 (p. 94). This document can be used as the basis of a periodic review.

Ten key strategies

Regardless of where the proposal to establish a partnership originates, there are certain strategies that schools and external agencies can employ to help to ensure that the principles outlined above are realised in action. These are set out in Figure B1 below.

---

1. Review the school's management arrangements.
2. Review the university's award-bearing framework.
3. Provide teachers with materials to support planning, reflection and leadership of development work.
4. Establish a support group/programme.
5. Provide opportunities and support for networking.
6. Design a structure for portfolios of evidence.
7. Provide participants with external critical friendship.
8. Provide participants with access to literature.
9. Support internal and external publication of accounts of development work.
10. Devise monitoring, evaluation and research strategies.

Figure B1 Key strategies for partnerships to support teacher-led development work

We now explain each of the ten strategies in detail.

Strategy 1: Review the school's management arrangements

Teacher-led development work is likely to flourish when certain conditions exist. The head teacher or principal may have the power to take the school into a partnership arrangement, but the impact of the teachers' work will be minimal if the management arrangements are not conducive. We recommend therefore that, as the school enters into such a partnership, the senior management or leadership team undertake a review which asks the sort of questions set out in Figure B2 below.

> ➤ To what extent do teachers have the opportunity to discuss their personal development priorities with a senior colleague?
>
> ➤ What part do teachers play in establishing the school's development priorities?
>
> ➤ To what extent do middle and senior managers have the skills to negotiate development priorities with their colleagues?
>
> ➤ What is the scope for teachers to exercise leadership?
>
> ➤ What structures exist to enable teachers to share good practice?
>
> ➤ What are the opportunities for teachers to collaborate with their colleagues to improve practice?

Figure B2 Reviewing management arrangements

The literature on school improvement and educational leadership provides a range of other tools that can be used to extend such a review (e.g. MacBeath and McGlynn 2002). It is important for the senior management or leadership team to consider the possible impact of teachers' development work and to take a careful strategic view. They will need to decide how much of the school's funding can be committed to any support arrangements and therefore how many of the school's teachers can be invited to participate. They will also want to consider whether to specify particular categories of teachers to participate, e.g. middle managers. In our experience, one of the strengths of groups established in schools to support teacher-led development work is that they tend to be cross-hierarchical and include teachers from all levels in the school.

Strategy 2: Review the university's award-bearing framework

In the UK, most university education faculties provide award-bearing courses for teachers. They would probably all claim to support school improvement, but it is perhaps less common for them to provide award-bearing structures which make such improvement the primary concern. In a partnership to support teacher-led development work, the university involved may need to review the structure of its accreditation framework – the design of the Certificates, Diplomas, Master's degrees and so on – and if necessary adapt it to make it more directly supportive of such work.

Universities' awards are usually governed by a document – sometimes referred to as 'the regulations' or 'the validation document'. It is this document which specifies matters such as the content to be taught and the assignments to be submitted. Below we have selected a number of key dimensions of such a specification in order to show how a framework might need to be adjusted to make it more supportive of teacher-led development work.

Table B1 Adapting the accreditation framework

Specification	Adaptations to support teacher-led development work
Time: the length of time that participants must be registered on the programme, the completion dates of the component modules, courses and assignments.	Participants' progress through the accreditation pathway is negotiated so that completion dates make a good fit with the progress of the development work being led by the teacher concerned. Flexibility is built in to allow for changing circumstances.
Content: the content of the programme – in terms of knowledge, understanding and skills – to be covered by all the participants.	The specification does not define a common content to be covered, but instead there is a description of the process through which participants identify their priorities, devise strategic plans, lead development work and reflect on the issues arising.
Assignments: the nature of the 'coursework' or assignments to be completed and submitted for assessment.	The 'coursework' requirement is the submission of portfolios of evidence arising from the writer's own leadership of development work or case studies based on those portfolios. The focus of each 'module' would of course be determined by the shifts in personal development priorities.
Assessment criteria: the assessment criteria against which the assignments will be judged.	Assessment criteria should emphasise reflection on strategic action (see example of assessment criteria in Resource 2, p. 95).

For the academic staff involved in partnerships to support teacher-led development work, there is likely to be a challenge to traditional patterns of work. Programmes that are based in a school or local professional development centre will involve university staff driving some distance and then working in an environment that may be less comfortable and not as well equipped as the accommodation at the faculty of education. Perhaps more fundamentally, academic staff will find themselves having to be responsive to the agendas of the participants and their schools rather than being able to focus on their own expertise. All of this may demand the provision of a programme of induction and support for those who want to take up this challenge.

Strategy 3: Provide teachers with materials to support planning, reflection and leadership of development work

At the heart of the proposals presented in this book is the idea that individual teachers can pursue their personal development priorities through a systematic, planned and reflective process. In order to sustain this process, teachers need a clear set of guidance materials so that they are not dependent on face-to-face contact with coordinators or external facilitators. This book should contain all that is needed, but it may be necessary to adapt the materials to suit a particular context.

In addition to the materials presented here, participants will need information about their particular context and programme. A pack of guidance material might include items such as those set out below.

Documents that specify:

> any special arrangements in the school for consultation about priorities and plans

> the university's assessment criteria

> the coursework requirements (assignments)

> library and other entitlements

> the arrangements for tutorial or external critical friend sessions

> the contact details of others in the group and/or network

> roles and responsibilities within the partnership

> the programme details (dates, times, content)

> a code of practice/ethical guidelines

> reading lists

Figure B3 Additional guidance material

Strategy 4: Establish a support group/programme

Although the reflective action planning approach has a strong independent dimension, it is nevertheless vital that teachers belong to a support group in which they can share their experience of leading development work and extend their professional knowledge. The group needs to be large enough to be cost-effective and to ensure a rich discussion in group sessions.

Any programme or scheme established to support teacher-led development work must be seen to be distinct from more traditional professional development 'courses'; partners and group leaders must resist labelling the group as a 'university group' or 'action research group', each of which carries unhelpful connotations. The group is primarily concerned with school development, learning and teaching and should be named accordingly.

Venue for the group sessions

If universities or LEAs are involved as partners, they may offer the university campus or the local authority professional development centre as a venue for group sessions. However, although there may be advantages in terms of the quality of the accommodation, the programme is likely to be much more accessible to teachers if it is located in a school. If the group sessions are held at the end of the teaching day it will be possible for teachers to incorporate their participation in the programme into their routine professional lives.

Funding the provision

A large secondary school may well be able to support a viable group with all the participants being drawn from that single school, but clusters of schools may wish to collaborate to provide a programme which moves from one school to another.

Alternatively, if a school has almost enough funding to be able to mount a programme, it may wish to 'sell' places to teachers in nearby schools. Those initiating a scheme could explore external sources of funding such as that currently available from the National College for School Leadership (the Networked Learning Communities initiative) in England (www.ncsl.org.uk).

Domestic arrangements

The importance of domestic arrangements must not be underestimated. The informal discussion that takes place over refreshments is a key part of the mutual support offered by the group and time should be allocated for this. Coordinators should aim to create an ambience that is conducive to reflection and discussion. Below (Figure B4) we suggest some *minimum* requirements to create the right sort of conditions for a programme.

> ➢ refreshments, food
>
> ➢ a room that is clean, tidy and pleasantly decorated
>
> ➢ appropriate furniture arranged to encourage discussion
>
> ➢ audio-visual equipment, flipchart, whiteboard etc.
>
> ➢ adequate heating/ventilation

Figure B4 Conditions for a school-based programme

These may seem obvious, but they can be overlooked. For example, it is not uncommon for the school heating system to be turned off when pupils leave the school, leaving teachers extremely uncomfortable at the end of a two-hour after-school meeting. Attention to details like these not only ensures people's physical comfort but also makes them feel valued. Occasional group visits (e.g. to the university library or a conference) and meals together can strengthen the group's identity. The importance accorded to these arrangements will affect the priority that participants give to their development activities. Poor quality provision will have a negative effect on teachers' commitment and therefore on the sustainability of the group.

Content of the programme

Joint planning involving both internal and external partners, and consultation with group members should ensure that the content of the programme is balanced. The content should reflect as fully as possible the range of interests within the group, drawing upon the expertise of group members and teachers from other schools as well as that of the external partners. There also needs to be a balance between the process (e.g. action planning, data gathering, managing change) and the specific, substantive content that the teachers may be interested in (e.g. assessment for learning, managing pupil behaviour, citizenship education). A facsimile programme is included in Resource 3 (p. 96). Figure B5 below contains an outline description of a typical programme.

> 12–15 two-hour 'twilight' sessions per year held at the sponsoring school

> a group visit to the partner university once a term

> jointly planned and led by an internal coordinator and an external provider

> content of the programme negotiated with group members

> guest speakers include teachers from other schools in the network

> seminars led by group members

> HEI lecturer brings material to supplement group members' inputs

> workshop activities to support the development process

> workshops in which participants discuss their development work

Figure B5 Typical features of a school-based programme

The ethical dimension

Real improvement stems from participation in a discourse that is both critical and authentic. This is likely to include sensitive issues and information about practice that might affect colleagues who are not members of the group. It is also likely to include personal disclosures which participants would not necessarily wish to share beyond the confines of the group. Confidentiality therefore has to be assured. Ethical principles should be agreed at the very beginning, written down in a formal code of practice (see Resource 4, p. 97 for an example) and discussed at regular intervals.

The code of practice should also deal with the ethical implications of data gathering in the school to protect the legitimate interests of colleagues, pupils and parents. Similarly, the implications of publishing accounts of good practice both within and outside the school need to be considered.

Strategy 5: Provide opportunities and support for networking

Of course it is perfectly possible for teachers to engage in development work as individuals, but in our experience this work is enhanced by belonging to a support group. Group leaders can ensure that the discussion is enriched by accounts of practice in other schools and by the findings of published research. However, teachers also need opportunities for dialogue with teachers from other schools, localities and systems. Contrast is a powerful tool for learning; it enables us to see what is distinctive about our own practices and, when we discover unfamiliar alternative ways of doing things, we are liberated from our taken-for-granted assumptions and encouraged to experiment.

We suggest a network with the features set out in Figure B6 below.

Clearly, the development of information technology and the world wide web has transformed the possibilities for networking, but successful networking seems to depend on some regular face-to-face contact. Not all network members will be able – or indeed willing – to participate in conferences, particularly if they are held on a Saturday or during vacation periods, but it is surprising how enthusiastic network members can become once they have experienced one or two really good conferences. See Figure B7 (below) for a list of features for successful network conferences.

In the organisation of such conferences, a balance has to be struck between the stimulation that might be derived from hearing keynote speakers and the benefits of sharing of experience in workshop situations.

> face-to-face conferences at least three times a year
> a regular newsletter, bulletin, or journal in hard copy
> a web site that includes:
>   - chat rooms and online conferences
>   - links to other networks and web sites
>   - online library searching
>   - bulletin board
>   - online journal/newsletter
> provision of information about network members –
>   their current development work and contact details
> links with other networks including international networks

Figure B6 Features of a network

> keynote presentations from well-known researchers and policy figures
> structured discussion sessions for sharing experiences and mutual support
> plenty of space and time for informal contact and dialogue
> publication and celebration of network members' work
> access to the university library
> coaching on skills such as library searching
> a bookstall
> opportunities to make arrangements for further networking
> updating of information about network members

Figure B7 Features of network conferences

Managing the network

Clearly, a network of this nature has to be coordinated; conferences have to be arranged, materials prepared. This may best be undertaken by the university, LEA, school district or other external agency involved in the partnership as they are more likely to have the necessary resources. The coordinators of the school-based groups may wish to form a management group to undertake the coordination tasks. Alternatively, teachers within the network schools could be asked to act as network coordinator in rotation, or the network conferences could be hosted by each school in turn.

At the time of writing, the National College for School Leadership is stimulating the formation of networks through the offer of funding. In order to qualify, schools have to commit themselves to supporting salaried coordinator posts. There is an important principle here: head teachers and principals need to commit resources to the formation of networks; networking activity requires considerable ingenuity and effort on the part of one or two individuals.

Strategy 6: Design a structure for portfolios of evidence

As a method of documenting professional activity, portfolios of evidence are versatile and can support authentic professional and organisational learning. They can also satisfy the academic requirements of a university. Portfolios can serve a number of purposes as indicated in Figure B8 below. The partners should design a structure that meets a number of such purposes in order to avoid duplication and to derive maximum benefit.

Portfolios can . . .

> enable teachers to reflect systematically on the progress of their development work over a period of time;

> provide the basis of a review of progress with colleagues either in the context of peer support or performance management;

> provide evidence of professional development and achievement for the purposes of career development;

> be presented to be assessed as part of the requirement within an award-bearing framework such as a Diploma or Master's Degree.

Figure B8 Purposes of portfolios

Of course the question of the structure of portfolios is closely linked to Strategies 1 and 2 in that it raises questions both about the way teachers are supported by the management structures in their schools and about the scope of the university's 'coursework' requirements.

It may well be that a common format for portfolios cannot be achieved. One difficulty is that the evidence needed for performance management purposes has to be of the sort that could reasonably be expected from all teachers in the school, whereas the evidence needed for an award-bearing bearing submission may be of the type only generated by those who are prepared to embrace the idea of leadership of development work. Perhaps a solution might be a core structure with optional extras for those participating in a teacher-led development work programme.

Strategy 7: Provide participants with external critical friendship

A 'critical friend' is someone who does not hold power over the person they are befriending, but is trusted to be able to offer a critical perspective and feedback that may be challenging but is accepted as being supportive. The concept of critical friendship has a well-established place in the literature on school improvement (see MacBeath 1998 for example), although it has sometimes been usurped by school inspectors in accountability contexts. Some of the characteristics of critical friendship are set out in Figure B9 below.

Critical friends work through *dialogue* through which they:

> seek to understand the teacher's goals and needs
> offer a critical perspective on the teacher's work
> help to identify issues and dilemmas
> offer sources of evidence and/or expertise
> encourage collaboration and the sharing of ideas

Figure B9 The nature of critical friendship

In addition to providing critical dialogue, the critical friend also needs to be able to bring particular expertise to the relationship: expertise in the methods of school-based data gathering and evaluation, and familiarity with a broad range of educational literature.

We suggest that the university is well placed to provide critical friendship in the context of teacher-led development work because of the particular values and traditions that predominate in universities. This kind of dialogue is a normal part of the academic tutoring practice of university staff, who should be used to working within an ethical framework in which confidentiality is guaranteed. University staff are also likely to be committed to such values as the pursuit of independent thought, the promotion of criticism, the application of rigorous inquiry and the development of the capacity for argument.

Teachers leading development work need regular one-to-one support in order to ensure momentum and to foster critical reflection. In Figure B10 below, we set out the characteristics of a good one-to-one relationship between teachers and their university-based critical friends, referred to here as 'university tutors'.

> formal meetings 4–6 times a year
> informal contact through mail, email and telephone
> scheduled within the school day (using a supply or substitute teacher to release a number of teachers in rotation)
> prepared in advance by sending the university tutor a paper, plan or other document to read
> documented – what was discussed and any action points

Figure B10 The tutorial relationship

Additional critical friendship and valuable support can be sought from trusted colleagues within the school who share values and concerns.

Strategy 8: Provide participants with access to literature

Reading is essential, not just within award-bearing programmes because effective school improvement depends on clarity and coherence of thinking, the validity of conclusions drawn from data, the availability of fresh ideas and the findings of research and inspection. It is difficult for teachers to prioritise time for reading, especially if engaging in work rooted in practice or if their school or home is a long way from a university library. However, there are ways in which schools and their partners can support teachers in this respect as Figure B11 below shows.

> the school's staff library can be enhanced

> the university can provide a selection of key texts to be lodged with the school

> the university can provide a library induction session

> the university can provide longer-term loans and online renewals

> the university can provide remote access to electronic databases and search tools

> the programme can include a workshop to develop skills in online searching

> participants can be encouraged to collaborate and share resources

> participants can write reviews of articles/books to discuss at group sessions and network conferences

> useful literature can be publicised in a network newsletter or web site

> booklists can be circulated and articles on relevant themes recommended

> schools can provide additional time for a 'study day' including a library visit

---

Figure B11 Providing access to literature

It is important to dispel the myth that the literature only offers 'theories', that practical knowledge can only be acquired through experimentation with practice or through contact with other practitioners.

Strategy 9: Support internal and external publication of accounts of development work

Teacher-led development work can have a much wider impact than improvements in the teacher's own classroom. Teachers have an important role to play in the creation and transfer of professional knowledge which involves sharing knowledge both within the school and more widely through networking and publishing. In order for this to happen, forms of support for such publication will be required and a strong expectation on the part of colleagues in the school that the information will be shared in some way.

Internal publication

Each individual teacher's strand of development work should include strategies for reporting to colleagues and there can be no blueprint for this. Such strategies will depend on the nature of the initiative and the context in which the teacher is working. The schools involved may already have established procedures and strategies for disseminating ideas, for example, a staff bulletin board dedicated to accounts of 'best practice' or a pamphlet published at the beginning of each term.

However, as we argue in Part A, simple dissemination does not work. Good development work involves collaboration with colleagues through which ideas are shared and developed together through experiment. It may also involve the provision of professional development events for the whole staff or for particular teams. These activities need to be planned in order to enable colleagues to explore new ideas and reconstruct them for themselves.

External publication

The establishment of a network as described above together with a web site and newsletter, bulletin or journal will provide the means to share the experience and outcomes of teachers' development work between a number of schools. It is important to increase the impact of the work and to expose the emerging professional knowledge to the scrutiny of a wider pool of colleagues. This needs to be reinforced by the networking activities described above, moving beyond dissemination to aim for a tangible impact on colleagues' practice. Furthermore, the teaching profession as a whole can learn a great deal from the experiences of those who have engaged in systematic and rigorous development work; network coordinators and group leaders should provide support and encouragement for teachers to engage in the following (Figure B12).

> publish case studies on the network web site
>
> make presentations at the network conferences
>
> publish case studies on national web sites
>
> submit articles to professional journals and educational newspapers such as the *Times Educational Supplement*
>
> present papers at conferences
>
> present case studies in the form of chapters in books

Figure B12 Publishing strategies

This kind of publishing requires considerable confidence and a range of skills, but it is vital in order to enhance the professional voice. Not only does it make an essential contribution to what is already known about improvement, but it can also influence policy at a national level. It also gives teachers a great deal of satisfaction and a sense of fulfilment.

Strategy 10: Devise monitoring, evaluation and research strategies

Systematic review through monitoring and evaluation should be integral to any programme or initiative supporting teacher-led development work. This is the responsibility of all partners, but may be driven particularly by head teachers or principals of participating schools who need to exercise judgement about the way their funding is being spent, or by an LEA which may have initiated or sponsored the project. All partners should share concern that the scheme is making an impact on pupils' learning and building individual and organisational capacity.

A contract or memorandum of agreement would provide the main point of reference for monitoring and evaluation. Regular reviews should be held and arrangements, roles and relationships should be adapted over time in response and according to changes in circumstances.

Evaluation might focus on: (a) the framework of support, (b) the development and effectiveness of networking and (c) the impact of the development work.

(a) Evaluation of the framework of support

It is likely that external agencies will have their own quality assurance procedures, but these can be supplemented by specially tailored evaluation to fit the particular circumstances of the programme or scheme. The participants are the main source of information. The questions in Figure B13 provide a starting point for gathering evidence and can be adapted as appropriate.

> Are the practical arrangements for groups and individual tutorials working well?

> Do you have access to support and advice when you need it? Do you have sufficient guidance literature and information?

> Are you able to make use of facilities and resources (library, information technology . . .) on a regular basis?

> Do the group meetings strike the right balance between support for the process of your development work, discussion on issues of individual concern and focus on generic issues?

> How is the network supporting you in your leadership of development work?

> Is the school supporting you in your leadership of development work?

> To what extent are colleagues, other members of the school community and people beyond the school aware of your work?

> Are there any particular obstacles to your leadership of development work, or issues you would like to raise?

Figure B13 Participants' evaluation of the support

Groups may wish to build in regular review discussions, perhaps once a term, in which issues are raised and suggestions made as to how the support can be improved. Group reviews are also an opportunity for revisiting the purposes and ethical and procedural principles to consider whether changes need to be made.

Key issues from discussion may be fed into review within the partnership, for example if teachers comment that access to reading to support critical reflection is difficult, this may be addressed by providing more information about online facilities and sources. It is important to allow sufficient time for partners to consider these issues and plan accordingly, also taking into account any issues raised by the leaders and coordinators of the scheme.

(b) Evaluation of the development and effectiveness of networking

This is a very challenging aspect of the monitoring and evaluation of a programme or scheme. Obviously particular events such as conferences can be evaluated individually, and comments can be gathered from the group review as described above (Figure B13), but assessing the extent to which a network is supporting participants in their leadership of development work and the sharing and transformation of professional knowledge is extremely complex. It may best be approached by engaging someone, either involved in the programme (for example a coordinator) or employed for the purpose, to gather data about the extent of formal and informal networking activities and the ways in which they are considered by participants and partners to be supporting the development process. If this is planned in the long term, it should be possible to assess the extent to which there is growth or change in networking activity and to shape the support accordingly, for example introducing more online discussion as confidence grows and access improves. Comparison with other networks through collaborative research would strengthen this development process.

(c) Evaluation of the impact of the development work

This is the crux of the evaluation of any programme or scheme. Workshop 11 (p. 90) is a review exercise in which teachers use tools in Resources 39 and 40 (pp. 134–5) to reflect on the impact of their development work. This is considered in terms of the impact on pupils, on teachers, on the organisation and beyond the school. The results of this exercise can be drawn together to establish the collective impact of the group. The emphasis will, of course, be different depending on whether teachers are from the same school, from a cluster of schools that work closely together or from schools that are not particularly connected.

Stakeholders may wish to collect additional evidence under these headings to investigate further the nature and extent of the impact. This may be organised against predetermined success criteria, but a flexible approach is advisable since there are often many unanticipated outcomes. It is essential to include qualitative as well as quantitative evidence if the range of impact is to be accurately represented.

Partnerships should seek to mirror the process of development work followed by participants, in particular gathering and using evidence, experimenting with practice and managing change through collaboration. While review and planning may focus on the specific arrangements that have been established, it may also involve developing a more conducive climate within schools and adjusting the ways in which external agencies work so that teacher-led development can flourish in that particular context.

Case studies

The approach described in this book has been used in a variety of contexts in recent years. Some of these are illustrated by the following case studies.

Case study 1

The first case is sponsored by a single school, one of a number that have entered into a partnership with the local university to support groups of teachers who are all leading development work and who are registered for Masters degrees.

Case study 1: The Charles Dickens High School's Development Group

This is a well-established group based in a secondary school in the south of England. It began as a cross-hierarchical group of 12 teachers, including some quite new to the profession, two senior managers and several subject heads.

The senior manager with responsibility for staff development coordinates the group. He meets with the university tutor once a term to plan and review the programme. He reports to the senior management team to maintain the group's profile, provides critical friendship to group members and offers advice on the funding of development activities.

The group meets four times a term after school, with individual tutorials once a term built into the school day. Some members of the group attend network conferences held at the university once every term on Saturday mornings. This face-to-face contact with colleagues from other schools is highly valued but the network is also beginning to experiment with online discussion and video conferencing. One edition of the network journal was produced by the group, publishing accounts of their development work.

The group is now in its fourth year of existence; two members have successfully completed their Masters degrees but attend the meetings to support their development work and mentor less-experienced group members. Several people have withdrawn from the group due to pressure of work or family difficulties. Conflicting activities at school and personal commitments sometimes lead to low attendance, so there is concern about maintaining a viable group and the school may invite colleagues from feeder primary schools to participate.

Teachers involved with the group are fully committed to their role in the school development process. There are discussions about linking more closely to the school's performance management structure and also running sessions open to all staff.

Case study 2

This case involves a partnership between the university and an LEA to support individual teachers from a number of schools. The development work is entirely focused on themes identified by the LEA's educational development plan.

Case study 2: The Wessex School Improvement Programme

Wessex LEA has developed a partnership with the local university to support teacher-led school improvement focused on key themes within its educational development plan, including school–community links and boys' underachievement. Teachers were invited to participate in a support programme jointly led by tutors from the LEA and the university. There was sufficient interest for three groups to be formed.

Meetings are held centrally at the LEA's development centre and participants are also supported by tutors' visits to schools, supplemented by email and telephone contact. The groups meet separately to focus on their particular themes and merge for sessions on generic topics and issues, and for guidance and workshops on process.

The participants find contact with colleagues from other schools useful and would like to extend this by linking with other networks. They sometimes find that the timing of sessions is difficult – travel from the farthest parts of the area can mean a starting time later than the normal after-school session or missing afternoon lessons. Another problem is the lack of access to library facilities: the LEA has a professional development library but to use either this or the university facilities means more travelling time. Participants are being encouraged to use web-based resources and a 'reading day' at the university is planned for late in the summer term.

Although numbers have sometimes dwindled at meetings, there is a core of extremely enthusiastic teachers who are carrying out inquiry-based development work that is directly linked to improvements in school conditions and to enhanced pupil learning. The co-tutors are currently discussing strategies for communicating the work to all Wessex schools and for drawing more teachers into the programme.

Case study 3

This case is focused on a particular subject – modern foreign languages – and involves a university-based tutor experienced in research in this field working with a group of teachers from ten primary schools.

Case study 3: The Primary Modern Languages Project

In 2000 the government made funding available to support school-based research by teachers in the form of 'Best Practice Research Scholarships'. A group of ten teachers were each awarded grants of around £2,500 to investigate and develop aspects of the teaching and learning of modern foreign languages in primary schools. A university tutor leads the collaborative research group that meets centrally at the university and provides ongoing support to individuals by visiting their schools to advise and guide the research. The teachers are registered for a postgraduate Diploma.

Each teacher is focusing on one of ten strands of the research, for example 'special educational needs', 'assessment', 'information and communications technology' etc. The group support one another through paired visits to observe and discuss approaches. They also use some of their funding to employ a part-time researcher to conduct interviews (e.g. with teachers, pupils and parents) and to collect and process additional data from the ten schools taking part. The programme of meetings includes inputs on issues surrounding the teaching of modern foreign languages and generic issues such as the management of change. Workshops support each teacher in the process of inquiry-based development work.

The teachers are disseminating their 'work in progress' and the outcomes of the project to local and national audiences, e.g. at subject and research conferences and through professional journals. One teacher has been allocated one day a week as an 'advanced skills teacher' through a government initiative, allowing her to visit local primary schools to provide training and support based on her research. Others have formed a working group to improve primary–secondary transition in collaboration with the LEA.

Part C

A framework for teacher-led development work

The process of teacher-led development work can be expressed as a series of elements as shown in the diagram, Figure C1 below.

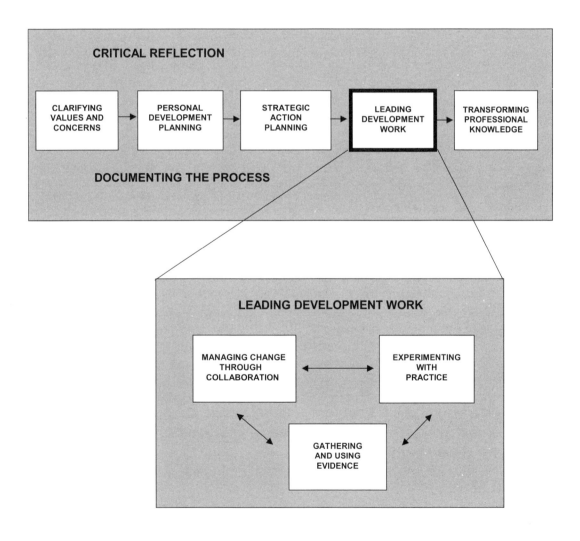

Figure C1 Teacher-led development work: a framework

Although the process that teachers follow is infinitely complex, expressing the elements separately enables them each to be explored in depth and the relationships between them to be considered. The systematic steps in the process – beginning with clarifying values and concerns and ending with transforming professional knowledge – can be followed for each episode of development work, although inevitably there will be some overlap of cycles of reflection, planning, action and evaluation. In the unpredictable environment of schools, the apparent linearity of the model will be compromised by changes in the circumstances and context of the development work, but the framework can still usefully be applied in order to maintain focus, direction and momentum.

The elements of 'critical reflection' and 'documenting the process' are shown as encompassing and supporting the process as a whole.

In this part of the book we introduce and explain briefly each element of the process. In Parts D and E we offer detailed guidance for teachers and those supporting them, followed by workshops (Part F) and resources (Part G). All these sections are based on the framework shown in the diagram above.

Critical reflection

Reflection is a natural part of teachers' everyday work, but more deliberate, rigorous and structured reflection, ideally involving writing, is essential for teachers who want to extend their capacity for exercising leadership. It helps them to plan and evaluate their development work, to make sense of its complexity and to develop fresh insights and perspectives on the issues. This becomes more critical with experience as practice is challenged and deeper understanding is sought about teaching and learning and the management of change. Opportunities for critical reflection should be planned by teachers and those supporting them as an integral part of the development process. Working with others (e.g. a critical friend, tutor or supportive group) makes this reflection more powerful in supporting professional and organisational learning and underpinning the process of change.

Documenting the process

To ensure maximum effect, teachers' development work needs to be explicit and visible to others in the school. Documenting the development work through written plans and the collection of evidence enables teachers to reflect on the process, evaluate it and review their own progress and achievement. It can contribute to the school's archive to support organisational learning about good practice and managing development work. Documents can be kept in a portfolio that provides a clear and accessible body of evidence of the achievements to date and of current plans, enabling individuals to maintain a clear sense of momentum and direction. It can also be used as the basis for reflection, consultation and review of the work in progress and as a summative record of achievement, perhaps linked to a formal performance management process. It can be submitted for the purposes of accreditation or used as a case record to support the writing of a more traditional dissertation if this is required.

Clarifying values and concerns

Successful development work requires the commitment and enthusiasm of individual teachers, so the process of identifying the focus for development work should begin with the individual's values and perceptions of the situation. Before entering into negotiation with senior colleagues about development priorities, individual teachers need to strengthen their conviction about those aspects of practice that need to be improved. The starting point should therefore be the individual teacher reflecting deliberately and systematically on his/her professional experience, values and concerns in a confidential setting. Positive and deliberate action to clarify values and perceptions enables the teacher to enter into the development planning process with confidence and clarity.

Personal development planning

Having clarified their values, responsibilities and concerns, teachers are in a better position to identify the way in which they are able to 'make a difference'. They can then produce a personal development plan – a statement setting out their personal development priorities – with which they can enter confidently into consultation and negotiation with senior managers and other colleagues. This ensures that the agenda for change is driven by strong personal commitment and concerns, but is also tied into and matched with school development priorities. In engaging in this discussion and negotiation, the teacher seeks a mandate for action and settles upon goals that are realistic. As the development work progresses, the personal development plan provides a useful basis for review and evaluation.

Strategic action planning

Following agreement about priorities, it is important to plan systematically the short-term action that needs to be taken to address development goals. The act of setting out intentions in the form of a written document that is made public within the school represents a firm commitment to action and encourages strategic thinking about how to implement change. Consultation with colleagues on the details of the plan can help in enlisting support, securing time and resources and setting realistic targets with dates for reporting and reviewing progress. Success criteria may be identified against which the outcomes of the development work can be measured. In the constantly changing school context, action plans are working documents reviewed and updated regularly to help keep the development work on track.

Leading development work

The successful leadership of development work flows from action plans that have been agreed by colleagues on the basis of negotiated development priorities rooted in the personal vision of individual teachers. It is helpful to think of the leadership of development work as having three interrelated dimensions:

1 Collaborating to manage change
2 Experimenting with practice
3 Gathering and using evidence

Each of these dimensions is dealt with separately below.

Leading development work: collaborating to manage change

Teachers are members of professional communities. Their development goals only make sense in relation to the goals of the school and the aims of the profession as a whole. Managing change therefore necessarily involves working with colleagues and consulting groups and individuals within the school, and interested parties externally. Those affected by change need to be kept informed, but even more importantly, they need to be engaged and involved so as to contribute actively to the development process and widen its impact. Genuine collaboration in which voices are heard and opinions and different perspectives are considered is more likely to lead to sustained change. Finally, a collaborative approach ensures that proposals and ideas are subject to the critical perspective of different professional audiences.

Leading development work: experimenting with practice

Development work is about changing practice and should be planned and negotiated with the expectation that change will take place. However, new practices cannot simply be imported from elsewhere – they need to be explored in the context of particular schools, teachers and classrooms. They will need to be adapted and modified to fit. Changes in practice challenge our beliefs and attitudes so we have to be prepared to exercise leadership. Evidence from within the school and from published research and inspection evidence can be drawn upon to support proposals for change, and systematic monitoring and evaluation will provide the basis for adaptation. Collective reflection on evaluation evidence will enable teachers to discover what works best in a particular context and increase their understanding of learning and teaching.

Leading development work: gathering and using evidence

The systematic use of evidence ensures that proposals for change have a sound foundation that is seen to be valid by colleagues and other members of the school community. Evidence can be drawn from published research, from data that already exists in school and from specific data-gathering activities. Inquiry can be integrated with everyday practice so that evidence is used as the basis for analysis, reflection and discussion to evaluate current practice and inform development work. Schools are increasingly 'data-rich' but it does not necessarily follow that these data are used effectively. The aim should be to develop a more systematic approach as part of the organisational culture of the school in order to enhance understanding of teaching and learning and of development processes. Furthermore, inquiry should be seen as a vehicle for managing change. It has the potential to empower people by enabling voices to be heard, perspectives to be articulated and proposals to be debated. In particular, working with evidence gathered from within the school has great potential to engage people, since it describes and illuminates their own experience.

Transforming professional knowledge

Teacher-led development work generates professional knowledge, i.e. information, understanding and skills. The individual teacher leading the development work increases not only their personal capacity, their stock of knowledge and skills, but also their capacity to engage in collaborative work. The development work can also impact on their colleagues' personal capacity and on organisational learning. Head teachers and principals have a clear responsibility to manage this process of 'knowledge creation and transfer' and to ensure that the school derives the maximum benefit from teachers' development work. Beyond the school, the stock of our knowledge as a profession can also be transformed through teacher-led development work provided that the teachers concerned are able to share what they have learned through networking and publication.

Leading development work in schools: a guide for teachers

This part of the book is intended for teachers who want to adopt a more systematic approach to leading development work in their schools. It provides detailed guidance on the step-by-step process described in Part C.

The text is organised into seven sections, one for each element in the diagram presented in Part C:

- Critical reflection
- Documenting the process
- Clarifying values and concerns
- Personal development planning
- Strategic action planning
- Leading development work
- Transforming professional knowledge

Each section includes the following elements: *rationale, activity, outcomes*. Teachers belonging to groups that support their leadership of development work can also use the linked activities and workshops in Part F (Workshops). Materials in Part G (Resources), including planning and information sheets and case studies, can be used by both individuals and groups to support the process.

Critical reflection

As Figure C1 (p. 23) shows, critical reflection is not a stage in the process but a continuous dimension of successful development work.

Rationale

Reflection is a fundamental human capacity that helps us to make sense of what we do and to make choices about what we do next and as such, it is part of your normal work as a teacher. However, in order to become more effective in making a difference, you need to adopt a more deliberate and systematic approach to reflection so that you can make sense of the complexities of your professional situation and challenge your ideas, assumptions and normal ways of working. This means that you have to make the time for reflection, create opportunities for it, build these into your professional life and make them part of your personal capacity. Solitary reflection is of course natural and unavoidable, but when you engage in dialogue, discussion and writing, you open up the possibility of becoming critical. Critical reflection begins with simple descriptions of what has happened, but moves beyond this to question the justification for what we do and challenge our beliefs and assumptions. The ability to bring about real change depends on this.

Critical reflection underpins all parts of the development process. At various stages there will be opportunities for a more intense episode, for example when you engage in a review with a senior colleague, when you are writing for particular audiences or for accreditation, or when you are preparing a report about your development work. Planning and action, consultation and negotiation should also draw you into collaborative reflection through the discussions and deliberations that arise in meetings, conversations, interviews, staff development events and so on.

Activity

Deliberate and systematic critical reflection begins with a consideration of your professional experience, concerns and values, and continues with reflection on and about your everyday practice and about the context and process of your work (see p. 33 'Clarifying values and concerns' in this section).

Beyond this, we suggest that there are three essential elements: (a) keeping a professional journal, (b) discussion with colleagues and critical friends and (c) writing a critical narrative.

(a) Keeping a professional journal

A journal provides the opportunity to record events and ideas as they happen and to deepen your reflective process. You can use the data to reflect systematically on your experience and on the process of leading development work.

You need to find a system that allows you to record events, conversations, feelings and issues as they arise. Your journal does not have to take the form of continuous prose in a notebook. You may work best using blank pages in your planner, pages in a ring binder, a computer file or a tape recorder in the car. You may want to fix a particular time of the day or week in order to reflect systematically, for example after particular lessons during which you have experimented with your practice, or you may want to make a note when you have something to record, for example after a significant meeting. You may devise innovative ways of noting and reflecting, for example through email correspondence with a critical friend.

Consider the purpose of your journal carefully. You could include notes on your inquiry process and reflections on your methodology so that it is more of a research journal (see Altrichter *et al.* 1993). You may decide to concentrate on setting down events with a commentary or to focus more specifically on your own professional learning. References to articles or books, quotations and other evidence that have helped to inform your thinking could be included.

(b) Discussion with colleagues and critical friends

Discussion is a form of collective reflection and your membership of a support group should provide opportunities for discussion in pairs, trios, small groups and in the whole group. These discussions should enable you to 'think aloud' and to receive critical feedback from your colleagues. One-to-one sessions with critical friends (see Part B) are also essential because in that relationship the critical friend has accepted the responsibility to provide that support and they will also have the advantage of continuity. They will be able to build up their understanding of your development work and the issues that have arisen over time.

(c) Writing a critical narrative

A narrative is a personal account of events, a commentary that tells the story; but selection and interpretation will naturally mean that it is not the whole story. The point is to identify the issues and reflect on them systematically and critically.

Adopting a 'critical' perspective means standing back from your experience and achieving a degree of scepticism, challenging your own ideas, beliefs, practices and interpretations. Evidence from experience and systematic inquiry needs to be accessible in order that the reader can check and challenge your interpretation.

The work involved in writing and refining a piece of critical narrative may seem daunting, but it is easier once you have a draft to work on – try to progress beyond the blank page as soon as possible even if you are unsure about what you are writing. 'Telling the story' is a good place to start. Your reading about the focus of your development work and leadership issues will provide insights to help you in the analysis and explanation of events and issues. This will enable you to make sense of your experience and to crystallise the professional learning that has taken place. Through your writing you will find that 'tacit' knowledge becomes explicit – you will become clearer about what has been achieved and what still needs to be done.

Draw on your journal, your memory and any documentary evidence you may have collected to help you to develop your story. The checklist below (Figure D1) will help you to decide what to include.

> the issues that have emerged in your development work
> (curricular, management, social, philosophical, political)
>
> your own professional learning and development, role and responsibilities
>
> your changing professional concerns and values
>
> anecdotes and informal observations that tell you about the impact of your development work
>
> future needs and targets for curriculum, organisational and personal development
>
> implications for school and wider educational policy

Figure D1 What to cover in a critical narrative

Some people find it difficult to imagine the 'voice' or style of critical narrative writing. In our own education we may not have been taught how to account for ourselves and our experience. Figure D2 below, provides a few guidelines to help you get started.

> write in the first person
>
> use clear and unambiguous terms
>
> avoid over-technical language and jargon
>
> avoid 'chatty' colloquial language
>
> refer to literature
>
> acknowledge sources of evidence

Figure D2 The critical narrative voice

You cannot approach this writing with the intention of being objective – your feelings and opinions are part of the whole picture and your account should be written in the first person. However, you do need to approach the task critically. Weaving together the evidence, the literature and your interpretation so that the reader understands the basis for the analysis is a subtle art that takes practice. Be prepared to share your writing early on in the process and accept comments and critique – this may be difficult to start with, but will help you to think and write more incisively and with confidence. Conversations based on critical writing can also be transformational, moving the development work forward as you reach a better understanding of issues and context.

Parts F and G provide workshop activities and examples that can be used by groups and individuals to develop critical writing skills (Workshop 2, p. 72; Resources 8, 9, 10, 11 and 12, pp. 101–6).

Outcomes

Ultimately, the most important outcome is your personal understanding, insight and awareness. Eventually you will get to know yourself and understand your school better, and gain insights into your own practice and the processes of school improvement. This professional learning is made explicit in the form of a critical narrative.

A critical narrative needs to be written at intervals. It may be appropriate to do this only once at the conclusion of a development project or initiative, but it is likely to be more powerful if written in episodes. It is assumed here that such a piece of writing will be written for the purposes of making sense of the experience of leading development work. The audience in the first instance may be the university to which you are submitting your portfolio for accreditation. You will need to check the university's conventions for format and presentation, including referencing.

Documenting the process

Documenting the process is about generating and collecting documentary evidence which, as with critical reflection, should be a continuous part of your development work as shown in Figure C1 (p. 23).

Rationale

Documentation throughout the development process is essential. It serves a variety of purposes as set out below (Figure D3).

> to provide a basis for reflection
> to be able to monitor progress
> to provide evidence for evaluation
> to inform future planning or next steps
> as a 'record of achievement' for those involved
> to provide a portfolio of evidence towards an academic award
> to provide a basis for review with colleagues
> to provide evidence to disseminate good practice
> to contribute to the school's archive of development activity

Figure D3 Why document the process of development?

30

A portfolio is the most useful vehicle for the documentation of your development work. This is a collection of separate items of evidence that would have been produced in the first instance for a variety of audiences and purposes. For example, the *audience* for an action plan is your colleagues and others involved in and affected by the proposed changes; its *purpose* would have been consultation and negotiation about your ideas and intentions.

Activity

There are two distinct but closely related aspects to this activity: (a) generating documentary evidence and (b) collecting it in the form of a portfolio.

(a) Generating documentary evidence

A great deal of development work takes place with very little being written down or evidence collected. The following story of development is not uncommon.

Development work without documentation

A teacher has attended a one-day conference about 'questioning techniques'. Following a conversation with the head teacher, she arranges a meeting with a group of colleagues to discuss the matter. In the meeting the teachers share their practice and explore the new ideas related verbally by the teacher who attended the conference. The group resolves to experiment with these new ideas and have further meetings to discuss the impact of this.

There is no doubt that this is useful and that the teachers concerned will have learnt from the experience, but the impact of this development work could be greatly enhanced if the work had been documented.

Development work enhanced by documentation

A teacher has attended a one-day conference about 'questioning techniques'. Following a conversation with the head teacher, she arranges a meeting with a group of colleagues to discuss the matter. In preparation for the meeting, the teacher produces a digest of the main ideas gleaned. In the meeting the teachers share their practice and explore the new ideas related verbally by the teacher who attended the conference. The team leader takes notes, recording which of the new techniques seem suitable for experimentation and the questions or issues surrounding their use. The group resolves to experiment with these new ideas and have further meetings to discuss the impact of this. The teacher who attended the conference offers to provide a framework that can be used by colleagues to keep a record of their classroom experimentation. This not only enhances the experimentation, but also generates useful evidence about the effects of the techniques. In subsequent meetings, the classroom experiences of the teachers are noted and used to produce a report for other teams in the school. The teacher who introduced the questioning techniques assembles all the documentation in a portfolio to be used for her performance management review and for accreditation purposes. An edited version of the portfolio is added to the school's archive so that subsequent development work can take account of this episode and build on it. This archive would of course be drawn upon in the event of a school inspection.

(b) Collecting documentary evidence

In order to preserve the evidence of the development work, you need to collect and store it in a ring binder or something similar. By evidence we mean artefacts or real documents that have been produced for professional purposes and for professional audiences. This includes planning documents such as your initial statement, personal development plan and action plans (as explained later, see p. 33–9), as these set out the foundation for the development work. They can be used to give structure to the organisation of evidence as the development work progresses.

Your collection of evidence is likely to include the types of evidence listed in Resource 13 (p. 107). It would be usual to organise these materials chronologically but you may decide that it is better to organise them differently, e.g. thematically. Talking through the evidence with a colleague or your tutor may help you to see more clearly the structure that might be appropriate.

This collection of evidence does not of itself constitute a portfolio; it will lack coherence and will not be intelligible to someone who is not familiar with the details of the development process and the context in which you are working. In order to create a portfolio, you need to organise and present the material. The way this is done will depend on how you intend to use the portfolio (see above and Resource 15, p. 109).

The particular design of the portfolio – the way it is constructed and organised – will be determined by your own style and creativity as well as your purpose, but there are some basic principles that will apply whatever the case. You can use Resource 16 (p. 110) as a checklist and review your progress with Resource 17 (p. 111), which can be used in Workshop 3 (p. 74). It makes sense to use any relevant guidance materials available in your institution, for example there may be a format for keeping a record of your professional activity to meet performance management requirements. To avoid duplication of effort, use your portfolio to serve a number of different purposes.

Outcomes

As explained above, we suggest that the documentation arising from your development is organised in the form of a portfolio.

Portfolios should include *evidence*, *commentary* and *critical narrative*; it is the careful and deliberate compilation of these elements that makes the portfolio coherent and intelligible to external readers, whether they are assessing for accreditation, reviewing your professional development or supporting you in your leadership of development work.

If you are presenting your work for accreditation you need to ensure that it is submitted in the appropriate format. Some accrediting bodies allow submission of portfolios with an element of critical commentary, but you may be required to submit a more traditional essay or dissertation. The portfolio of development work can still be used as the basis for this. Resource 18 (p. 112) explains how you might turn the sections of the portfolio into a dissertation.

Remember to retain the portfolio to use as a working document from which you can extract evidence and ideas to further your development work, to engage colleagues in the change process and to reflect on your personal professional development. The section on 'Transforming professional knowledge' (see p. 48) discusses how the knowledge you have gained may be communicated and contributed to organisational learning. Your portfolio can provide a good source of evidence for the school archive – an important aid to organisational learning. This is likely to require further selection and adaptation.

Clarifying values and concerns

This is the starting point in the process of systematic, teacher-led development work.

Rationale

If you want your development work to make a real difference, it needs to be focused on something you feel strongly about – something that arises from your own values and concerns. You need a great deal of conviction to sustain the momentum when the process of improvement becomes difficult – as it inevitably does. This is not to say that your development priorities should spring only from your personal values and concerns without reference to the school's agreed priorities, but before entering into discussions with senior colleagues about the contribution you might make to development work in the school, you need to be clear about what you think is important. You can then negotiate with confidence.

For this reason, it is important to begin the development process by reflecting deliberately and systematically on what might be called your 'professional predicament', i.e. your situation, circumstances and concerns. This is not as straightforward as it might sound; you may be surprised to discover how powerful it can be to take a little time to sit down and think this through. This reflection works best if it is done with the help of colleagues but in a confidential setting. It involves clarifying your current responsibilities and professional situation, but also delves deeper into your professional values and your perceptions of which aspects of practice could be improved. An important part of the reflection is the drafting of a written statement, an activity which is of itself reflective and can lead to fresh insights. The document should remain private and should only be read by a trusted critical friend, one of your colleagues or a tutor within an academic context.

Activity

There are two stages to this part of the development process: (a) a collaborative reflection exercise and (b) the writing of an initial statement.

(a) A collaborative reflection exercise

You need the opportunity to talk to someone about your professional situation and your current responsibilities, interests and concerns. This could take place within the support group to which you belong or within the context of performance management, appraisal or mentoring in your school. You may want to ask a colleague to act as a critical friend especially for this purpose. Figure D4 provides a structure for this reflection.

> Professional history

> Role/development last year

> Issues arising from last year

> Role this year

> Consultation within school

> Strengths and needs

> Values and interests

> Hopes and aspirations

Figure D4 Headings for clarifying values and concerns

Workshop 4 (p. 76) features an interview-style exercise designed to support this reflection, while Resources 19 and 20 (pp. 113–14) provide a format and prompt questions for use either in the workshop or in any other suitable situation.

(b) Writing an initial statement

Having talked it through, you need to reflect on your own and write something down. With the support of a tutor, mentor or critical friend, you should draft and redraft a statement which represents as accurately as you can the way you see your 'professional predicament'. This should *not* be a public document shared with senior managers or other colleagues unless you decide that it would be helpful to do so; rather it should be for private reflection – something that helps you to think through your concerns and priorities.

Outcomes

The most important outcome is that you should be in a much stronger position to frame your personal development priorities and to enter into negotiations with colleagues about your personal development plan. This important reflection should be made explicit in the form of an initial statement.

Figure D4 can be used to help you prepare your initial statement; Resources 19 and 20 are only guides. You may feel more comfortable with different headings and should feel free to structure your statement in a way that suits your particular circumstances and your individual writing style. Resource 21 (p. 115) may help you to imagine the sort of document that is required.

It is suggested that a statement of between 1,000 and 2,000 words should allow for the necessary detail. This document should be included in a portfolio of evidence to enable you to keep track of the development process. It could provide a basis for review at an appropriate point in the future.

Personal development planning

This section is about constructing a personal development plan and negotiating with colleagues.

Rationale

Having clarified your values and concerns by writing an initial statement, you are better placed to be able to identify your *personal development priorities*. This term does *not* refer to priorities for your personal or professional development; it refers instead to the way in which you can contribute to development work in the school. Such development work can have a wide range of effects or impact as we describe below. Clearly, if these priorities are concerned with change and improvement in your school, they need to be negotiated with your colleagues – in particular with those who have management responsibility. A personal development plan that emerges from effective consultation is likely to be successful in leading to sustainable school improvement.

Activity

There are three stages to personal development planning: (a) identifying personal priorities, (b) consulting and negotiating with colleagues and (c) writing the personal development plan.

(a) Identifying priorities

First you need to reflect on your values and concerns, and then analyse the situation in your own school. The school may be in a position to use self-evaluation tools (see for example MacBeath 1999; MacBeath and McGlynn 2002) or tools for diagnosing the school's culture as described in Part E of this book (see also Hargreaves 1999). If this whole-school approach is not practical, you may want to use such tools on your own or within your team – they can also be explored within your support group. Your colleagues are more likely to be persuaded of the value of your proposed development work if you have evidence arising from the use of such tools.

(b) Consulting and negotiating with colleagues

You need to discuss your priorities with a range of colleagues including those with senior management responsibility; they will probably have better knowledge and understanding of whole-school priorities as well as a range of other factors that will affect your decisions. You need to assess the extent to which your proposed development work fits within the school's agreed priorities and with the prevailing organisational conditions in the school. You can use the checklist in Figure D5 below.

> match with school priorities
>
> potential to affect teaching and learning
>
> degree of 'leverage'
>
> synergy with other initiatives

Figure D5 Factors affecting the choice of focus

We suggest that you use the checklist in discussion with your colleagues to ensure that the focus for development is one that is likely to bear fruit and has the support of your colleagues. Particularly important is a consideration of 'leverage' which is concerned with an assessment of the likely benefits of a strand of development work in relation to the energy and time it will demand. The aim is to refine your ideas so that your plan will represent a clear mandate for action and a sound basis for review and evaluation of the development work at a later stage.

(c) Writing the personal development plan

Unlike your initial statement, your personal development plan is a document intended to be shared with colleagues for the purposes of consultation. It therefore needs to be written in clear and precise language and should be very brief (no more than a few paragraphs). You can structure it using Resource 24 (p. 118). Your plan should set out what you believe you ought to be working to develop over the coming year. The scope of the plan will depend to some extent on your position or role, but it may be that you want to go beyond the normal expectations of your position because of a particular concern or interest (see Resource 23, p. 117).

You should show drafts of your plan to colleagues – particularly those with managerial responsibilities – and use members of your support group as sounding boards. Workshop 5 (p. 77) features discussion about the nature of personal development plans and the process of deliberation and negotiation through which you can identify your development priorities. Workshop 6 (p. 79) will help you to envisage the outcomes of your development work so you can plan more effectively. Discussion may be needed to explore how certain areas of impact might be achieved, for example you may need to talk to the head teacher about how your work might be used to support your colleagues' professional development since you may need time and funding for collaborative work.

Your plan may go through several drafts before it accurately represents your agreed development priorities. It should provide a clear sense of direction although the path of your development work is likely to change direction as it unfolds and the context changes.

Outcomes

A personal development plan should be the culmination of a process of consultation and negotiation which ensures both clarity about your aims and maximum support from colleagues.

Figure D6 (below) indicates the kind of headings that are likely to be useful in writing a plan, but you need to devise a format that is most appropriate for you. You may like to consider a format that fits with other documents such as the school development plan or the school's professional development portfolio. If another planning document serves the same purpose, there is no need to write two plans – simply copy the appropriate document into your portfolio of development work.

> Roles and responsibilities
> Focus for development
> Development priorities

Figure D6 Personal development plan format

When your plan has been agreed you can add it to your portfolio, but you may also want to include earlier drafts so that you can reflect on the way your priorities were shaped by the process of consultation.

Strategic action planning

This section is concerned with the action plan(s) that will help you to pursue the goals set out in your personal development plan.

Rationale

Having agreed your development plan you need to consider in more detail how to pursue your development priorities over a particular time span. Development work will tend to unfold in unpredictable ways – it will be shaped by the opportunities that arise and by the sometimes unexpected responses of colleagues, pupils and other stakeholders – but it is more likely to be successful if it is well planned in the first instance.

Written action plans enable you to consult stakeholders and seek advice and support from both colleagues and external critical friends. They will provide a clear point of reference for future action and a useful basis for monitoring and evaluation as the development proceeds. However, action planning is not a one-off task – it is a process in which you try to imagine the most strategic way forward. It therefore needs to involve consultation and negotiation to ensure that the resulting plan matches the circumstances and has maximum support from colleagues. It may be wise to conduct a preliminary analysis or investigation before drafting the plan in order to assess the obstacles and opportunities. The plan should be a brief and concise written document that can be readily understood by colleagues. It should:

- describe the action you will take;
- outline the strategies for collaborating or engaging with colleagues;
- illustrate the opportunities for experimenting with practice and the data-gathering strategies you will use to evaluate or inform the development work.

Activity

We have identified three elements to this activity: (a) consultation and reconnaissance, (b) drafting the action plan and (c) negotiation.

(a) Consultation and reconnaissance

In thinking through your strategy you will need to consult with colleagues and to weigh up the factors set out below (Figure D7).

In thinking about your strategic plan, consider the following:

> links with other initiatives

> the micro-political terrain

> the leadership conditions

> the provision of external support

> the organisational structures and processes

> the prevailing organisational culture

Figure D7 Considering obstacles and opportunities

These headings form the basis of an instrument that can be used to structure this consultation and 'weighing up' (see Resource 28, p. 123). You may want to work on this with a colleague from the senior management team or perhaps a critical friend.

You will also need to consult your external critical friend or university tutor, particularly with regard to the data-gathering aspects of the plan. The point here is to make the inquiry dimension of the plan as rigorous as possible.

(b) Drafting the action plan

A good action plan summarises the focus for development, then sets out the events and activities that you believe will result in improvement. You need to set realistic targets with dates for reporting and reviewing progress. Action plans should reflect key dimensions of leading development work:

- managing change through collaboration;
- experimenting with practice;
- gathering and using evidence.

These are explored in more detail in 'Leading development work' below (pp. 39–48).

The structure of your action plan will depend on the specific nature of the development work to which you have committed yourself. Since the document is intended to be shared with colleagues, it needs to be written in a concise and accurate style.

Suggested headings for an action plan are set out below (Figure D8) and a fuller version is also included in Resource 31 (p. 126).

> **Focus for development**
> *The development priority or aspect of it, the context*
> **Proposals for change**
> *New practice, implementation, classroom experiment, the expected outcomes*
> **Collaboration and consultation, reporting**
> *What, with whom, when?*
> **Evidence-gathering strategies**
> *Questions/issues, data needed, instruments and techniques*
> **Targets and timescales**
> *What and by when?*
> **Evaluation and review**
> *With whom, when?*
> **Outcomes/impact**
> *In relation to development priorities*

Figure D8 Strategic action plan

An example of an action plan is included in Resource 29 (p. 124).

Workshop 7 (p. 81) features a whole-group discussion of the nature and elements of action plans, and a small group activity designed to enable you to develop action plans that adequately address your agreed personal development priorities.

(c) Negotiation

When you have a first draft of your action plan you will need to consult with a range of colleagues and seek their agreement about the details of the plan. This is not just about seeking permission, it is also about seeking support. You could use the checklist below:

> Does the plan require any additional resources?
> Does the plan conflict with any school policy or code of practice?
> Will the activity disrupt teaching?
> Will the activity involve visits from people outside the school?
> When could colleagues expect a report on the development work?
> Is it necessary to dedicate time on the calendar for training events?

Figure D9 Negotiating an action plan

It is important that the plan is as strategically sharp as you can make it and that you have been able to identify both obstacles and opportunities. However, it is also important that you have a mandate to lead the development work your plan encapsulates.

Outcomes

The tangible outcome of action planning is, of course, an explicit written action plan that has been shared with colleagues. Your action plan will probably need to be adjusted in the light of experience; you should keep all versions because they document the work and will help you to reflect on the process. Annotation or an accompanying commentary can record these changes just as well. Your plans can be used as a personal checklist of what has/has not been achieved and for review with colleagues. They can be included in your portfolio where they can be cross-referenced with other relevant documents.

Leading development work

Clearly this is the major part of the process – it is the whole point of the exercise. Leading development work necessarily involves a commitment to being a 'change agent'. Initiating a process of change will inevitably highlight tensions between colleagues and bring into sharp focus differences in values, beliefs, attitudes and approaches to classroom practice. This is clearly a considerable challenge for which you need to be prepared.

Workshop 8 (p. 83) will enable you to explore the relative importance of a variety of leadership tasks. Sorting and prioritising these tasks will allow you to explore the challenge of leadership and the extent to which your leadership style meets that challenge.

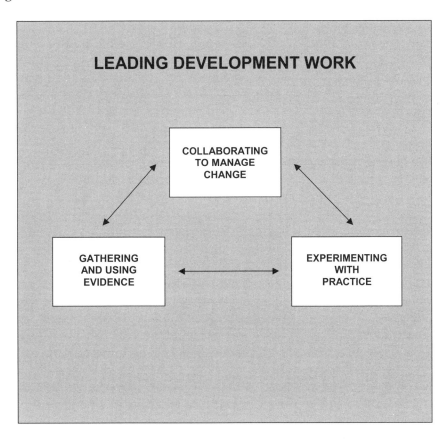

39

As explained in Part C, it is helpful if you think in terms of these three key elements in leading development work: (a) managing change through collaboration, (b) experimenting with practice and (c) gathering and using evidence. However, it is important to view the development process as a *balance* of these elements. Integrating them leads to what Mitchell and Sackney (2000) call 'profound school improvement'. So, while we will look at each of the three elements separately, we want to emphasise that this is a somewhat artificial distinction and that they should be seen as aspects of the same process. We consider the outcomes of this integrated process on pp. 47–8.

Managing change through collaboration

A critical part of your action plan will be to identify strategies for collaboration.

Rationale

If your individual leadership is to be powerful, there must be a strong and direct link between your personal development priorities and those of the school. It follows that collaboration should form a continuous thread running through the development process. Figure D10 below sets out the arguments for a collaborative approach.

> to ensure that the initiative is accepted by colleagues
>
> to ensure that the development work is adapted to the particular context of your school
>
> to mobilise support, help and resources
>
> to contribute to colleagues' professional development
>
> to have impact on the learning of the greatest number of pupils
>
> to have impact on the school's organisational capacity

Figure D10 Why collaborate?

Your development work has the potential to have impact in a wide variety of ways (see Resource 27, pp. 121–2), but this potential will only be realised through collaboration with colleagues.

Activity

Even if your development work begins in your own classroom, you should consider ways to maximise its impact by drawing colleagues into the process at an early stage – don't wait to disseminate. Work with colleagues, students, parents and others to investigate practice and devise new strategies. Think creatively about your use of time with colleagues and make it as interactive as possible, allowing people to voice opinions, ideas and concerns, give feedback and plan collaboratively. Encourage people to share ideas and experience so that together you can identify and build on existing good practice. Your development work will gain momentum and become sharper if you expose it to the scrutiny of different interest groups. This may mean challenging the culture and working to make it more collaborative. Workshop 9 (p. 85) helps you to think about your school's culture and how to engage with the school as an organisation.

The activity of managing change through collaboration could be examined under a number of headings.

(a) Consulting colleagues and stakeholders

Clearly, the whole point of writing explicit personal development and action plans is to be able to consult with interested parties, potential collaborators and those whose support you need to be able to sustain the development work and overcome obstacles. This is often a matter of sitting down with individuals and groups to talk through a plan and being prepared to adjust it in the light of those discussions.

(b) Keeping colleagues and stakeholders informed

Consultation should not be seen as a one-off event but rather the beginning of an ongoing process. Development work can run into difficulties if colleagues and others become afraid that it is unfolding in ways which threaten established interests. In any case, the development work will fit better into the context and become embedded if stakeholders' views, knowledge and experience are taken into account.

(c) Establishing special interest groups

It is now commonplace in many schools to establish some kind of group to focus on an aspect of development. For example, a working party on 'assessment for learning' may bring together a small group of colleagues with an appropriate range of expertise, pivotal positions in the school and a degree of enthusiasm to carry out research and development over a particular time span. In many cases schools will establish a group with a more general brief such as 'teaching and learning' or 'school improvement'. As a leader of development work you may want to consider establishing a group to focus on your concern. Alternatively, you may want to ensure that your concern becomes part of the agenda of an established group.

(d) Working within teams

In most schools, teams are a more or less permanent feature of the organisation. In secondary schools, teachers will tend to belong to a subject department or a pastoral team; in a primary school, it may be a key stage team or year group. Teams such as these provide perhaps the most obvious opportunities for collaboration such as joint planning activities or evaluation exercises.

(e) Establishing partnerships within the school

Development work can be advanced by teachers forming partnerships for mutual observation, mentoring, coaching or other data-gathering activities. For example, the science department may agree to carry out a comparative investigation with the art department as a way of exploring the links between teaching styles and subject matter.

(f) Working with pupils

Increasingly teachers are exploring opportunities to collaborate with students through a variety of strategies for accessing the 'student voice'. For some this is a matter of establishing focus groups so that students' views about teaching and learning can be heard, but in some schools students have been more actively engaged as researchers, posing their own questions and gathering data to address them.

(g) Whole-staff development activities

Whole-school development days present opportunities for the presentation of new ideas by inspirational speakers, but such events are most effective when they include structured reflection and evaluation exercises. They also offer ideal opportunities for teachers to present data and engage their colleagues in considering the implications for practice.

(h) Establishing partnerships beyond the school

Contrast is a powerful tool for learning and collaborative arrangements to pursue development work in two or more schools can be extremely beneficial. In England, Beacon School status has provided additional funding to support such inter-school collaboration and the recent launch of the Networked Learning Communities initiative provides substantial support for such work.

Experimenting with practice

A critical part of your action plan will be to identify strategies for experimenting with practice in classrooms and elsewhere.

Rationale

Development work is essentially about change and improvement in practice resulting in improvements in pupils' learning. It is about discovering 'what works' through practical experimentation.

It is true that teachers have always improved their practice in an experimental way, but for maximum effect this needs to be more systematic than the trial and error intrinsic in normal everyday practice. Strategies for improving pupils' learning need to be tried, tested, evaluated and refined.

As we argued in Part A, knowledge about 'what works' cannot simply be imported – it has to be tried out in practice, adjusted and adapted to fit the particular teachers, classroom, students and school. The national reform movement has tended to emphasise the somewhat simplistic idea of 'implementation' rather than development, but changes in practice involve far more than the adoption of a new set of materials or even a new set of classroom strategies; they usually require the acquisition of new skills and can also demand a fundamental rethink about values and beliefs. This means that time has to be allowed to develop new practices and an environment has to be created in which colleagues feel safe to take risks.

In order to maximise the extent to which change will be embedded you need to draw colleagues into the process so that learning about practice is shared. Changes in your own practice individually or within a small group of committed colleagues need to be shared as widely as possible within the school. The success of the new or improved practice depends on being able to make it visible and demonstrate its benefits.

By sharing accounts that are accessible and convincing you can draw others in, starting with those who are most interested and receptive, thereby increasing confidence and building a momentum for change.

Activity

The guidance in this section is organised around a number of key strategies as set out in Figure D11 below and explained subsequently.

> creating an environment for risk-taking
> joint planning
> improving by incremental steps
> evaluating in action
> mentoring and coaching
> making good practice visible

Figure D11 Key strategies for experimenting with practice

(a) Creating an environment for risk-taking

Looking at real professional practice can be threatening, but if we are really interested in improvement we need to be able to look at what we do as teachers in classrooms and elsewhere. It follows therefore that you need to create the conditions within which colleagues feel relaxed about being observed, and giving and receiving feedback that is sufficiently robust to make a difference. One way to help to create these conditions is to discuss the ground rules and agree on who shall observe, who can see notes, what kind of judgements can be made and so on. Another way is to ensure that any observation is mutual or reciprocal. More fundamentally you need to build trust within a team – this is a matter of the quality of relationships and dialogue.

(b) Joint planning

The best way to work on the problem of safety to take risks is through joint planning. If members of a team have been involved in working out which aspects of practice to experiment with, how this can be observed and evaluated in action and how this will feed back into joint decision-making, there is likely to be a high level of ownership and commitment to the enterprise. Joint planning will also lead to a more intensive dialogue about practice through which groups of colleagues develop their understanding together.

(c) Improving by incremental steps

Our experience and evidence suggests that improvement is more likely to be sustained if change is incremental. When a team agrees to focus on something manageable such as 'the way we clarify the learning objectives at the beginning of lessons', there is a greater possibility that colleagues will be able to concentrate on that practice and gather useful data that can be used to refine and embed good practice. Large-scale, sweeping change can often lead to confusion, demoralisation and rejection.

(d) Evaluating in action

Judgements about what works cannot wait for the next round of the results of national tests and examinations – they need to be based on other kinds of evidence of wider learning outcomes. In order to determine whether or not a practice is worthwhile, we need evidence that can be extracted from data such as classroom observations and pupil feedback (see 'Gathering and using evidence' below for more detail). There may well be plenty of persuasive evidence from published research, but changes in practice have to be looked at in their particular contexts.

(e) Mentoring and coaching

Changing practice involves the development of our professional skills. It is not simply a matter of choosing to do something differently and then implementing a practice. Rather, it may be a matter of colleagues trying out new practices, observing and working with each other to learn how to get it right. Some versions of coaching imply that it is something carried out by those with expertise to benefit those without it, but we suggest that this is simplistic and that it is more productive to see it as a mutual or reciprocal activity.

(f) Making good practice visible

In order to capture what we learn through practical experiment we need to make good practice visible beyond the small group of people actually involved in the experimentation. Concise, accurate and rich descriptions of good practice will enable you to widen the involvement and draw colleagues into the experiment. They will also add to the school's stock of professional knowledge (see also 'Transforming professional knowledge' on p. 48).

(g) Gathering and using evidence

Your action plans should reflect the intention to gather and use evidence to inform the development work.

Rationale

Evidence is vital in the development process. Proposals for change are more powerful when supported by evidence, particularly when it is derived from data collected from within the specific school context. Data can also be used to assess the impact of development work and the effectiveness of different strategies. More than this, though, inquiry can be used strategically in managing the change process, for example inviting people to engage with different kinds of data encourages them to become more involved in the development process.

You need to develop a critical and creative approach to evidence gathering, to ensure that it is rigorous but at the same time wholly appropriate, manageable and relevant to your work as a change agent. The need to meet the academic criteria of a Masters degree may appear to suggest inquiry modes that are unhelpful; it is vital not to lose sight of your development priorities and the link between evidence and practice. Your primary reason for gathering data and the use of the evidence they provide should be to support a process of development that leads to better teaching and learning. The academic programme or scheme you are registered with should support such an approach.

Figure D12 (also Resource 36, p. 131) suggests some ways in which evidence might be used and the questions it might help to answer.

> **To identify or clarify a problem**
> *What is the problem and what is the extent of it? What is likely to be the best course of action?*
>
> **To examine alternative practice**
> *What do observation and accounts of others' practice tell us about our own?*
>
> **To monitor and evaluate classroom practice**
> *How effective are our teaching strategies in helping pupils to learn?*
>
> **To validate proposals for change**
> *What are the potential benefits of change?*
>
> **To adapt a new practice to fit your situation**
> *How are ideas from elsewhere fitting into the unique characteristics of our own classroom or school and how might they need to be modified?*
>
> **To give voice to colleagues, students, parents and other stakeholders**
> *How can we use evidence from different perspectives to shape policy and practice?*
>
> **To monitor the process of development**
> *What can we (the school) learn about leading and managing change?*

Figure D12 Using evidence

Activity

The modern school is a 'data-rich environment'. Much information and evidence already exists that can be used to provide the basis for development work. Inquiry and development work should involve a continual flow of information, ideas and action. Much data is created as a matter of course and simply needs to be identified and collected. In addition to this, you may also need to plan particular episodes of data gathering such as a series of interviews with pupils or colleagues, or some classroom observations. All this data can be used to inform the development process or to evaluate and refine your actions. You should also be collecting evidence to document the development process itself in the form of development plans, minutes of meetings and so on (as explained in 'Documenting the process', above).

Do not be too ambitious in your data gathering and in the amount of evidence you will be trying to interpret. To begin with, it may be helpful to investigate within just one class or with a small group of pupils before considering how the knowledge and understanding you have developed might be applied more widely by you and your colleagues. There is plenty of literature available to guide your data gathering and analysis: time should be set aside within your support programme for discussion and guidance on this aspect of your leadership of development work.

It is vital that you use data-gathering methods that can easily be built into day-to-day routines. The gathering of data should not be allowed to interfere with teaching. Figure D13 below suggests some strategies for integrating it into everyday practice (see also Resource 37, p. 132).

> **Use evidence that is already available**
> *For example, test scores, minutes of meetings, professional development portfolios, pupils' work . . .*

> **Use creative strategies for collecting evidence**
> *For example, group interviews with pupils, discussion groups of staff with a spokesperson to report back, a videotape of a lesson, emailed comments from pupils at the end of their homework . . .*

> **Investigate a range of techniques**
> *Besides the ubiquitous questionnaire and individual interview, through selected reading about teacher research and action research*

> **Plan time to discuss the evidence with colleagues**
> *Request time during existing meetings, bid for a slot on a development day, etc.*

> **Keep a journal**
> *Collect ideas and reflections on the inquiry process as you go along using for example, a tape recorder in the car, notes in the margin of your planner . . .*

> **Get practical help**
> *A university research student? An adviser from the LEA or school district? A parent? A governor?*

Figure D13 Strategies for integrating evidence gathering with everyday practice

There are a number of key issues that you will need to consider as you plan and carry out evidence-gathering exercises:

- Rigour
- Ethics
- Analysis
- Interpretation

(a) Rigour

Consider the validity (accuracy and truth) and reliability (extent to which it is replicable) of the data and make use of techniques such as triangulation (using data from a number of different sources). Use the research methods literature to widen your understanding of the issues, but be aware that much of it is written by university-based researchers and may not necessarily address the context of teacher-led development. Subject the evidence to the scrutiny of others – particularly your school colleagues – to test your interpretations.

(b) Ethics

Consider ethical issues in collecting evidence and reporting to others in the intense environment of the school. Colleagues, students and others have an entitlement to be protected from any harm that might arise from gathering evidence about practice or performance. This has to be balanced with the right in a public institution to subject practice to scrutiny. Enlist the support of your external critical friend or university tutor in clarifying purpose and process and in working through the issues that arise.

(c) Analysis

Consider the strength of the claims you can make and the limitations as well as the strengths of your 'insider perspective'. While analysis happens all the time through your engagement with the data and involvement in the situations you are investigating and seeking to change, you will need at times to move to a more formal analysis in order to make sense of the data in their entirety.

(d) Interpretation

Avoid regarding data analysis as simply a technical process. Bear in mind that theoretical and moral judgements are needed to select evidence and that you and others are involved in the interpretation, the telling of the story, the making sense of the information available. In order to use your evidence strategically you need to seek meanings and understandings rather than results.

Ideas about the strategic use of evidence gathering are developed further in Workshop 10 (p. 88) using Resource 38 (p. 133). If you and your colleagues are engaging with evidence with a clear focus on learning and teaching, this will increase the school's capacity to use evidence more consistently to direct, support and evaluate change and to introduce more practice that is genuinely evidence-based.

Outcomes of leading development work

Development work demands a considerable amount of time and energy so it is important to be able to judge whether there has been sufficient payoff. As an individual, you need to know whether the sort of development work you have been leading was worth the effort you put in, while your school needs to develop its organisational wisdom so that the right sort of development work is encouraged and supported in the future.

We have tried at various points in this book to broaden the idea of impact. It was recommended that at the planning stage, Resource 27 (p. 122) could be used to focus on a wide range of possible outcomes. As the development work proceeds – and certainly as it comes to some kind of conclusion – you need to reflect on its impact and take account not only of those outcomes that were planned and envisaged but also those that were unintended and unanticipated.

Figure D14 below is a reminder of the ideas about impact set out in the 'Planning for impact' tool. These are expressed in a different way in Resources 39 and 40 (pp. 134–5). You may also find Resource 41 (p. 136) helpful in envisaging outcomes. We recommend that you use the resources both individually and in your support group to evaluate your development work. Draw upon your journal as a reminder of events and issues as you reflect on what has been achieved.

> **Impact on pupils' learning**
> *Attainment, disposition, metacognition*

> **Impact on teachers**
> *Classroom practice, personal and interpersonal capacity*

> **Impact on the school as an organisation**
> *Structures and processes, culture and capacity*

> **Impact beyond the school**
> *Policy debate, professional knowledge, community growth*

Figure D14 Outcomes of teacher-led development work

Reflecting on the outcomes will help you to write a critical narrative which makes sense of the development work. Look back at 'Critical reflection' (above, pp. 29–30) for guidance on writing the critical narrative.

The next section deals in greater detail with strategies for achieving greater impact.

Transforming professional knowledge

This section is about contributing to the growth of professional knowledge both within the school and the wider professional community.

Rationale

Your development work will have resulted in gains in professional knowledge for you, your colleagues and your school. Through your reflection on the outcomes of the development work, and through the writing of your critical narrative, you will have become clear about what has been learned. However, it may be that more can be done to spread that knowledge both within and beyond the school.

There is enormous scope for sharing and learning to take place between schools – and you may also be able to contribute to wider educational discourse, for example to policy development and research. This may seem far-fetched or grandiose to those who feel that the professional voice has been diminished by years of 'top-down' reform, but we suggest that it is time for teachers to recognise that they have the expertise and that they are best placed to develop professional practice by testing out ideas in classrooms and schools.

The extent to which your development work is of wider benefit depends largely on the extent to which you can rise to the challenge and take responsibility for sharing what you have learnt. We suggest that participating in a programme of support for teacher-led development work should provide a context within which you can make your voice heard. You need to take advantage of the opportunities that arise and work creatively, collaboratively and strategically to find ways to maximise the impact of your work.

Sharing what you have learnt is by no means straightforward. A simple dissemination process may put information in the public domain but does not pay any attention to what happens to the knowledge once it has been reported, whether in oral or written form or on a web page. We know from experience that application does not automatically follow. Inviting colleagues to engage with the information, for example through a seminar discussion or workshop on a staff development day, may be more productive. The drawback to this is that it may be a one-off event; due attention needs to be paid to how people might use the information to develop their own practice, to *transform* the knowledge in their own professional contexts through active and interactive processes.

Activity

The case study, Resource 42 (p. 137), demonstrates a range of ways in which it is possible to share professional knowledge within and beyond the school. The guidance set out below corresponds to that learned from the case study and is organised under the headings listed in Figure D15.

> clarifying what you know

> making it visible

> strategic internal publication

> drawing colleagues into the conversation

> collaboration with other schools and networks

> publishing

Figure D15 Sharing professional knowledge

(a) Clarifying what you know

As we said at the end of 'Leading development work' (above, p. 26), you need to reflect systematically on the outcomes of your development work and use your critical narrative as a vehicle for clarifying what you have learnt.

(b) Making it visible

You need to rework accounts of your development work, adopting different styles according to your intended audience and the purpose of the account. You should develop a straightforward and accessible basic writing style – remember also that editing and layout are essential skills in the information age. Busy professionals do not have the time to read long and esoteric dissertations, so you need to be able to describe practice and highlight the key messages concisely.

(c) Strategic internal publication

You will need to consult senior managers in the school to discover the most effective means of communication. It may be a live presentation at a development day, an entry into a weekly bulletin or a briefing paper to a team of middle managers. Whatever the case, the choice should be influenced by the question of how the information is to be followed up.

(d) Drawing colleagues into the conversation

Experience tells us that simple dissemination is ineffective. Colleagues may read a paper or listen to a presentation, but they are unlikely to act on it unless there is a context or ongoing strategy that demands a response. So you need to think strategically about an activity that will create the need to know about whatever it is you want to share. This may well be a review of their practice in the light of particular proposals, or it may be that colleagues are asked to comment on a new policy arising from your proposals.

(e) Collaboration with other schools and networks

If you participate in a programme of support that has a strong networking element (see Part B), you will find yourself easily drawn into information sharing and other collaborative activities with teachers from other schools in the network. Like Richard (Resource 42) you may find yourself asked to act as a consultant, coach, mentor or a provider of a workshop or presentation as part of a training programme. The extent to which this happens may depend on the effectiveness of your strategies to publish accessible accounts of your development work.

(f) Publishing

The academic journals present a considerable challenge to teachers who wish to publish accounts of their work, although many editors are keen to publish articles by practitioners. However, there are many other outlets such as web sites and professional magazines which are not subject to the academic refereeing system. Where partnerships to support teacher-led development work are well developed (see Part B Strategy 9, p. 17), it may be possible to bring together accounts of development work in book form.

Outcomes

The outcomes of such knowledge-sharing activities are hard to measure, but it is clear from anecdotal evidence that they make a major contribution to the growth in organisational capacity in schools and networks. The profession as a whole is moved forward through the accumulation of practical wisdom gained from teachers' development work, which is informed not only by the fruits of professional university-based research but also, crucially, by teachers' own evidence-based experimentation.

For those who take up the challenge of teacher-led development work there are substantial rewards. In our research (Frost and Durrant 2002b), teachers talk about a radical transformation of how they think about their work as teachers and how participation in this kind of process has led to career development and a raising of their morale.

In the final analysis, we suggest that teachers need to articulate their professional voice through the creation and sharing of professional knowledge gained through the leadership of the sort of development work described here.

Supporting development work in schools: a guide for external support

This part of the book provides guidance to help coordinators, facilitators, mentors, consultants, advisers and university tutors to plan programmes and activities to support teacher-led development work. The sections follow the same structure as Part C and should be used alongside the corresponding sections in Parts D, F and G. We have included an additional section ('Introducing the support framework') in this part to discuss the induction of teachers into a support group.

The elements of the process discussed in each section (and represented in Figure C1, p. 23), will need to be returned to over time in order to deepen understanding of the process of leading development work.

The support should be thought of in terms of a 'spiral curriculum' that is primarily concerned with process. As a support group becomes established, those who are more experienced may act as mentors or critical friends to those who have newly joined, and may assume leadership of parts of the sessions to build the capacity in the school, group of schools or area.

Each section in this part of the book is organised under the headings:

- Rationale
- Supporting the activity
- Presentation and accreditation

The ideas and materials offered are not intended to form a complete set of resources for a support programme, but to illustrate the kinds of materials and activities that can be used and to provide a starting point. Group leaders will need to collect other resources and develop their own ideas. It is important to ensure that the programme is developed in response to the circumstances of particular schemes and the needs of groups. The challenge for group leaders is to maintain the freshness and relevance of the programme for participants while continually reinforcing the process.

Introducing the support framework

This section provides guidance for those who are responsible for supporting and leading a group of teachers who have elected to participate in a scheme to support teacher-led development.

Rationale

Once a partnership has been established to support teacher-led development work in a school or a number of schools, the recruitment and induction of teachers needs to be carefully planned in order to make a decisive start, build enthusiasm and capture the imagination of participants. This is the point where the basic principles and philosophy of the programme or scheme have to be clearly conveyed – any misconceptions should be dealt with from the outset. Depending on the prevailing culture, interested teachers and members of their schools will bring ideas from their own experience that can be built on or, if necessary, challenged. It is vital therefore that partners have worked through the principles as suggested in Part B and established a firm philosophical basis for the programme or scheme before starting to introduce the ideas to the teachers. It is most important at the start to establish the idea that everyone can make a difference within their own professional situation and that this approach is designed to support that aim.

Supporting the activity

Any group supporting teacher-led development work will need to begin with an introductory session to explain the approach, set out the supporting framework and establish the principles of the group and its work. This should include all the practical arrangements, for example library access and network conferences and communication (see Part B). Ideally representatives of the partnership supporting the group – including the head teacher or principal – should attend this initial session. Sharing the leadership of the session sends out a powerful message that partners share responsibility for the support and are fully committed to the project, rather than it being externally delivered.

Workshop 1 (p. 70) provides an outline for a session that enables the group's co-leaders to present the approach in context, and to allow participants to respond and explore issues and implications. Following an initial presentation, it may be wise to allow teachers time afterwards to consider whether or not they wish to participate, since the success of the scheme depends on strong individual commitment and motivation. The practical details will need to be explained fully, for example, how much time will be involved and over what period, the location of the meetings, the requirements of the accreditation and what facilities and resources are available.

If teachers are already involved in review and appraisal, development planning, action planning, using evidence, collaborating, documenting and leadership of development work, it would be wise to adapt the supporting framework offered here to combine with current practice, thereby rendering it more powerful.

A presentation from a teacher with experience in leading development work who has participated in a programme of this kind would be helpful. Ideally this should be someone currently working in a similar school or area with which teachers in the new group can identify – someone who might inspire the teachers to think of themselves as change agents.

Group co-leaders should allow time for a planning meeting to take into account the issues raised by participants so that the arrangements are tailored as far as possible to needs. It is vital that all those involved have accurate expectations and understandings about the group and the programme or scheme that supports it.

Once membership of the group is established, a letter or bulletin could be distributed listing contact details of participants, coordinators and group leaders, and setting out arrangements such as dates, times and locations of meetings. It is important that administrative arrangements are properly in place so that the programme or scheme runs smoothly and energy can be channelled into support for teachers' leadership.

Critical reflection

Critical reflection underpins the whole process of teacher-led development work. This section should be read in conjunction with the guidance for teachers (Part D, pp. 27–30).

Rationale

Reflection is an integral part of the exercise of professional judgement. We would not be able to function in terms of minute-by-minute decision-making without what Schon (1983) called 'reflection in action' to inform our actions and judgements. If planned systematically, reflection can be developed into a powerful tool to increase teachers' critical perspective on their practice and the complexity of the school context.

The process of clarifying values and concerns helps to strengthen individuals' resolve and develops their ability to articulate ideas and challenge thinking and practice. Subsequent collaborative work creates opportunities for collective reflection, which increases understanding as the development work progresses. As we argued in Part A, the development of organisational capacity depends on sustained critical reflection – not only by individuals but also collectively in different contexts, groups and interactions within the school community.

Formalising reflection through writing – both during the process and at particular stages of the development work – clarifies and deepens understanding. The writing can then be used as the basis of further discussion.

Through reflective writing, subjectivity is not only accounted for but embraced and used to help to explore the dynamic of change. Reflective writing can be as influential as other forms of data in challenging and stimulating others' thinking, since it is usually authenticated by their own experience in which they will look for parallels and contrasts. If one person makes their tacit knowledge explicit, this can prompt discussion of collective understandings and help to move the development work forward. Critical writing needs to be based on the teacher's reflection on their experience of leading change, but it will be more powerful if it draws upon the evidence accumulated in the portfolio and on relevant literature.

Supporting the activity

Supporting the growth of capacity for critical reflection is a gradual process and should respond to individual need. The first stage is to support the discussion of values and concerns and the subsequent writing of the initial statement; this is explained fully in 'Clarifying values and concerns' (p. 56).

(a) Keeping a professional journal

This can be introduced following the 'Clarifying values and concerns' exercise (Workshop 4, p. 76). It is worth spending some time in the group session discussing various ways of keeping a journal and what might be included in it. Resource 8 (p. 101) may be helpful in exploring this. It may also be useful to link this with Resource 27 (p. 122).

(b) Discussion with colleagues and critical friends

In order to develop the school's organisational capacity you need to build capacity for critical reflection within the support group. This will eventually affect the quality of discussion and reflection throughout the school. As often as possible the workshop activities should use techniques that require participants to support each other's reflection, for example in pair work or in trios. Establishing a code of practice early on will help to create the conditions in which participants can reflect on their values, concerns, practice and personal capacity. These activities will build intra-personal capacity (Mitchell and Sackney 2000).

Group leaders should also provide one-to-one tutorial support which we suggest should be seen as a form of critical friendship (MacBeath *et al.* 2000). This suggests a dialogue in which the participant is able to discuss a wide range of issues concerned with their development work, as well as the more obvious issues concerned with the development of their portfolio and related academic concerns. There are clear advantages to the critical friend role being undertaken by the co-leader from the university: they are not involved in the internal micro-political world of the school and can therefore be non-judgemental on many issues. They are also likely to have a clearer grasp of the requirements of the academic award that the teachers are pursuing. However, this is not to say that critical friendship cannot be provided from within the school (see Holden 2002a).

(c) Writing a critical narrative

The 'Clarifying values and concerns' stage of the process should lead to the writing of an initial statement, which is probably the first step towards critical narrative writing. This should establish that writing in the first person is not only permissible but necessary in order to consider values, personal priorities, experience and meaning. The facility to write in this way needs to be cultivated throughout the programme so that participants are able to look back at the evidence accumulating in their portfolios and to construct a critical narrative that is analytical. Workshop 2 (p. 72) can be used to develop the facility for critical writing.

Presentation and accreditation

As explained in the 'Critical reflection' section Part D (pp. 27–30), the initial statement and subsequent critical narratives should be included in a portfolio of evidence submitted as part of the requirement of an academic award. If a dissertation is required, this material can be incorporated as shown (see Resource 18, p. 112). It is important to make participants fully aware of the requirement and the attendant presentation conventions early on to avoid the necessity of making adjustments later. As we said in Part B, assessment criteria may need to be developed to ensure that credit is given for the kind of writing that will also be useful to support the development process (see Resource 2, p. 95).

Documenting the process

This is the second of the two continuous features of the process of teacher-led development work as shown in Figure C1 (p. 23). See also 'Documenting the process' in Part D (pp. 30–2).

Rationale

The vignettes presented in part D (see also Resource 14, p. 108) demonstrate the value of generating documentation. An essential part of knowledge management is the cultivation of the habit of making practice visible so that the organisation can share professional knowledge, learn from mistakes and accumulate the wisdom on which school improvement depends. So much of our professional practice remains at the tacit level which stands in the way of organisational learning.

The documentation of development work needs to become habitual so that selections can be made from the materials collected. These materials can be used to support collaborative work, to contribute to a school archive, and for the purposes of reflection, review and evaluation. A selection can be compiled for the purposes of the submission of a portfolio towards an academic award. The documentation can enable teachers to chart the progress of strands of development work and to explore the process of change.

Supporting the activity

The vignettes mentioned above can be used as the basis of a discussion about documenting development work and organisational learning.

The process of documenting the complexities of the development process is not as straightforward as it might appear. A manageable system is needed to ensure that evidence can be selected and stored systematically without expending too much time and energy. It is likely that teachers will only be able periodically to sort, select, sequence and review the materials they have collected, so it is helpful to provide time and structured activities within the programme such as Workshop 3 (p. 74).

It is suggested that materials are selected and presented in the form of a portfolio of evidence that can be used for a range of professional purposes (see Resource 15, p. 109). Issues that surface may include the nature of evidence and what kinds of evidence are valid, how to select evidence, labelling and organisation. Individual support in which the evidence is worked through in detail with a tutor/critical friend is invaluable.

If a portfolio is to be submitted for accreditation, participants will need guidance in writing a commentary and accompanying critical narrative to achieve the necessary levels of depth and criticality. Labelling and cross-referencing are crucial and the finished document will need to be bound carefully since it may contain materials in many different formats. If a more formal or traditional format is required for accreditation, clear guidance will be needed on how to adapt the portfolio and incorporate writing that has been completed in the course of the development work. Resource 18 (p. 112) shows how a portfolio including the various elements outlined in this book can be converted into a dissertation with sections or chapters. A careful selection of evidence and authentic documents can be included in the appendices.

Ensure that account is taken of institutional systems and structures that are already in place. When compiling evidence and commentary, bear in mind how evidence is used and how organisational learning takes place. This is considered in more detail in 'Transforming professional knowledge' below (p. 65).

Presentation and accreditation

If the development work is to have impact beyond individuals' practice, the materials assembled should be considered primarily in terms of how they can contribute to wider professional knowledge and understanding, and to the school's institutional archive charting particular development strands and processes of change (see 'Transforming professional knowledge' below, p. 65).

It is important to preserve a distinction between a teacher's collection of evidence and any portfolio or report that they might produce. The individual teacher should retain ownership and control of the material (see Part B, Strategy 4, p. 13 and Resource 4, p. 97). Due consideration must be given to ethical issues, e.g. in making public particular evidence or personal reflections that relate to individuals or groups within the institution.

If development work is to be accredited in the portfolio format it may be necessary to devise specific criteria to ensure that it is assessed appropriately both in relation to its format and to the award in question (see Part B, Strategy 2, p. 9 and Resource 2, p. 95). A less traditional style and format should not be used as an excuse to sacrifice the quality and rigour of the thinking and writing.

Clarifying values and concerns

This is the first stage of the process described in Figure C1 (p. 23). This needs to be read in conjunction with the guidance for teachers (Part D, pp. 33–4).

Rationale

At the beginning of the development process, individuals need to develop greater clarity about ways in which they can contribute to school improvement. They need to develop their confidence and strengthen their conviction in order to be able to enter into consultation and negotiation about priorities. They may be working with colleagues who have considerably more power and authority within the school. Senior colleagues will of course have a clearer view of the school's overall development priorities, and there is a danger that this view will simply be passed on without any real attempt to reconcile the teacher's view of what matters with the school's development agenda. This is perhaps particularly prevalent if the school is under pressure to implement externally imposed reforms.

Anthony Giddens's structuration theory is helpful in illuminating the way 'bottom-up' power can be exerted to change the structures that shape our actions (Giddens 1984; see also a discussion of Giddens's theory in Elliott 1998: ch. 9). This perspective assumes that there is a dynamic tension between 'structure' and 'agency'. Change can occur when teachers' agency is enhanced so that it can challenge the structures that may constitute obstacles to improvement. We argue in Part A of this book and elsewhere that teachers' transformative capacity – their capacity to 'make a difference' – can be developed by helping them to become clearer about their values and interests, and therefore, their own concerns and priorities. By providing a framework for 'personal vision building' (Fullan 1993) we can enhance teachers' capacity to play a fuller part in the professional discourse that shapes practice in their school. Reflection and clarification of individual values and concerns strengthens the individual's bargaining position as they enter into negotiation with their senior colleagues about priorities for development.

Reflection is more powerful if it is structured and systematic. It is not sufficient to ask teachers simply to go away and reflect on their values and concerns – their busy lives are focused on teaching and tasks associated with it. A great deal of teachers' professional knowledge is tacit so we need to create the scaffolding that supports this discourse. Reflection of a profound and sustained kind is supported through writing. We are often faced with negative attitudes to writing on the part of some colleagues but our experience suggests that this is because so much of the writing that teachers have been required to do in academic contexts has been seen to have little practical value.

Supporting the activity

There are two stages to this part of the development process: (a) a collaborative reflection exercise and (b) the writing of an initial statement to support private reflection.

(a) The collaborative reflection exercise

This can be facilitated in a number of different situations but is best done at the very beginning of a programme as a workshop for a teachers' group (see Workshop 4, p. 76). Resource 19 (p. 113) should be used in pairs or trios to enable each participant to reflect on their 'professional predicament'. The blank format (Resource 20, p. 114) can be used to make notes to provide a basis for the initial statement (both Resources 19 and 20 can be adapted to suit the circumstances of your group).

(b) Writing the initial statement

It is important to build on Workshop 4 by asking participants to draft a written statement. Some may need considerable encouragement and support. It is not unusual for teachers to feel daunted at the thought of resuming writing after a long break, or to lack confidence in writing in a way that might conflict with their taken-for-granted view of 'academic' writing. The style of writing may be more reflective and personal than anything they have previously tackled, and it may appear at first glance to lack intrinsic value. Use the example of a teacher's initial statement (Resource 21, p. 115) to discuss the 'voice' appropriate for such a document.

You will need to remind participants that the initial statement is a *private* document that plays an important role in the development process; it does not have to withstand the scrutiny of colleagues but it does need to be sufficiently detailed, structured and reflective to serve the purposes outlined above. The group leader should collect these statements and make a critical response; several drafts may be necessary to produce a polished document. This can be used as the basis for a review of professional learning and progress as the development work proceeds.

Presentation and accreditation

The initial statement is a suitable introductory item in a portfolio. It should demonstrate the ability to write reflectively and critically, identify and discuss educational issues and present coherent arguments and ideas.

Personal development planning

This is the second stage of the process described in Figure C1 (p. 23). This needs to be read in conjunction with the guidance for teachers (Part D, pp. 34–6).

Rationale

After a period of detailed personal reflection, participants need to look outwards in order to set their development work firmly within the context of school development priorities. Communication with colleagues at this early stage is essential if the work is to gain support within the institution in order to have the intended impact. It is vital that participants engage in work that will impinge on the institution, affect others and result in change.

In addition, the nature of the development priorities adopted will determine whether or not the development work has the potential to contribute to the development of the organisational capacity of the school. Both the participating teachers and their senior colleagues need to develop their awareness of the potential of such work. The case study, 'Andrew's story' (Frost *et al.* 2000: 94–107), illustrates how a relatively junior member of staff can, through effective consultation with senior managers, make a very significant contribution to school development.

In relation to individuals' development priorities, recent research in the school improvement field indicates that some foci are more fruitful than others, and that overload and multiple initiatives constitute obstacles to effective improvement processes (Gray *et al.* 1999). It is argued by David Hargreaves (2001) that development goals should be set with the idea of maximum 'leverage' in mind. Leverage is about the maximum benefit for the minimum input in terms of time, energy and materials.

Supporting the activity

It is important that the head teacher or principal and the co-leaders of the support group discuss the question of how those in formal leadership positions in the schools can support the process of teacher-led development. The review outlined in Part B (see Figure B2, p. 9) may be extended by a discussion of the guidance offered in Resource 22 (p. 116) which will focus discussion on the concept of leverage.

(a) Identifying personal priorities

The 'Clarifying values and concerns' exercise (Workshop 4) should have helped participants to understand more clearly the contribution they can make to development in their school. Now they need to translate this into a statement about their priorities and goals. Workshop 5 (p. 77) will be helpful in enabling participants to share their ideas about priorities and develop confidence in expressing them succinctly.

Teachers are likely to need help in imagining the full range of potential impact the development work might have on pupils' learning, teachers' capacity and on the school as an organisation. Use Workshop 5 (p. 77) and Resource 27 (p. 121) to open up discussion on the question of impact.

When trying to clarify development priorities, participants may be tempted to ask you, as their external critical friend, about the suitability of their focus. It must be made clear that it is inappropriate for an external tutor, mentor or critical friend to make a judgement about this; they can support individuals in thinking through a range of possible priorities, but the judgement about their priorities has to be the product of consultation and negotiation with the teacher's colleagues in the school.

(b) Consulting and negotiating with colleagues

Strategies for negotiation and consultation can be suggested to encourage participants to seek opportunities to enter into dialogue with colleagues at an early stage. As suggested above, it is the responsibility of the head teacher, principal and others in senior management roles to ensure that the proposed development work is likely to have a good 'effect size' or high leverage (Hargreaves 2001) and that, if necessary, the teacher leading it is protected from their own enthusiasm.

Group leaders should prepare both the school managers and participants for the process of consultation and negotiation. Draft statements about development priorities need to be honed and rehearsed within the safe environment of the support group so that participants can approach their senior management colleagues and others with confidence. The final development plan that emerges should be one that has been accepted by colleagues as being both legitimate and practical.

(c) Writing the personal development plan

The personal development plan should not be lengthy; it can be drafted during the workshop activity (see Workshops 5 and 6) and written up shortly afterwards. The example (Resource 23, p. 117) can be used to help participants envisage their plan. External critical friends can offer to give feedback on draft plans to ensure that they are clear. The final version can be lodged with senior colleagues as appropriate and used in the future as a basis for review.

Presentation and accreditation

The personal development plan and any additional planning documents, such as those that specify intended outcomes, should be included in the portfolio of development work and kept as an initial point of reference. These are useful documents upon which to base critical reflection on progress with the external tutor or in consultation with colleagues in school. Copies of personal development plans may also be kept centrally by the school to indicate the focus and scope of teacher-led development work linked to the school development plan.

Strategic action planning

This is the third stage in the process of teacher-led development work as shown in Figure C1 (p. 23) (see Part D, pp. 36–9).

Rationale

An action plan sets out the detailed steps teachers intend to take to address a specific development priority over a short timescale. By setting out their intentions explicitly in this written form and discussing it with colleagues, teachers can achieve legitimacy and support for the action that will flow from the plan. In addition the development work will achieve momentum because the plan will give rise to expectations from interested parties.

In the UK at least, we have plenty of experience of action planning within the school development planning process, but this may be limited to what tends to be referred to as 'implementation' rather than development. If a university is involved, there may well be a concept of a research- or inquiry-focused action plan, but this is also limited in that it serves primarily an academic purpose. By contrast, our interest here is with a plan that is inquiry-based but above all it is 'strategic', that is to say, focused on the leadership dimension.

The act of setting out intentions in the form of a written document which is made public within the school demands that participants think through all stages of the process and make a firm commitment to action. In our experience, this is very challenging for teachers who may not have experience either of inquiry or leadership, so tutors and critical friends need to provide positive support to plan for strategic intervention, taking into account the factors that can help or hinder the change process.

Supporting the activity

First it is important to make a clear distinction between the personal development plan – which sets out long-term aims and priorities, usually for the year – and action plans that break the development work into manageable stages and address the details of the action to be taken.

(a) Consultation and reconnaissance

Arguably, the first step in strategic thinking is reconnaissance. Obviously there can be no 'one size fits all' strategy because each school has its own particular history, culture and organisational identity. So the teachers participating in your programme need support to be able to assess the terrain over which their development work has to progress. Figure D7 (p. 37) derives from the Impact Project research (Frost and Durrant 2002b) in which we argue that development work is likely to be more or less successful depending on the conditions described and on the extent to which the teacher's action plan is crafted to respond to a realistic assessment of those conditions.

(b) Drafting the action plan

The format outlined in Part D is designed to help participants to structure their own plans, but it must be emphasised that the headings are only illustrative and they should be encouraged to use whatever headings with which they feel comfortable. What is important is that the plans reflect a balance between the strategic and inquiry dimensions.

The gathering and use of evidence will make the development process more powerful, so participants need to think about inquiry strategies specifically as they draft their action plans. All professional action carries opportunities for gathering ideas and information, seeking feedback, reflecting, analysing and evaluating as part of the interactive process of development. Approaching the work in this way enriches the process and ensures that inquiry is part of, rather than an addition to, professional practice and change management. However, it is essential to avoid seeing the action plan as being a plan for 'a research project'. The action plan is a statement of intentions regarding school improvement or curriculum development; it should include inquiry strategies that are necessary for that improvement or development to be as effective as possible rather than to satisfy the academic requirement of an award-bearing framework.

Workshop 7 (p. 81) can be used to enable participants to think through these issues and to achieve a balance between the three dimensions of leading development: (a) managing change through collaboration, (b) experimenting with practice and (c) gathering and using evidence (see Workshop 6, p. 79).

(c) Negotiation

Group leaders may well discover that teachers' attempts to negotiate with their colleagues can result in difficulties. For example, the intention to evaluate a classroom practice introduced by the deputy head just a year or two previously may create unexpected tensions. Similarly, a proposal to develop a literacy scheme which appears to run counter to the government-sponsored approach would have to be very sensitively negotiated with senior managers. Nevertheless, these difficulties have to be faced if the development work is to stand a chance of succeeding. Group leaders can help by creating space within the programme for rehearsal of the negotiations which are challenging but safe.

It is always necessary to revisit action plans and adjust them in the light of experience so group leaders will need to devise appropriate activities that allow participants to review their plans – perhaps during natural breaks in practice such as at the end of a term. Participants may be disconcerted by the organic nature of the development work as it grows and re-orientates in response to the changing school context, and the roles and circumstances of those involved. It is important to allow time to adjust to this.

Presentation and accreditation

Action plans are a crucial part of the evidence of the development process and can be used as the basis for a checklist of what has been achieved and what has still to be addressed. They should be included in the portfolio where they can be cross-referenced with relevant documents and evidence to support a critical commentary on the development process.

Leading development work

This is the major part of the process shown in the diagram below. You will need to be familiar with the guidance for teachers (Part D, pp. 39–48).

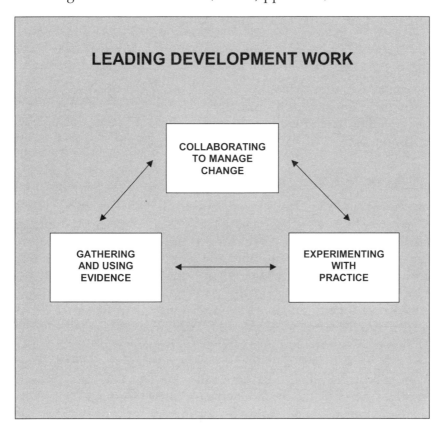

Rationale

There is a growing body of opinion and research that teacher leadership is the key to school improvement and capacity-building in schools (see Harris and Muijs 2002 for example). However, leading development work is different to the sort of leadership that comes with a senior or middle management responsibility in that the teacher has to take on the responsibility without the usual expectations on the part of colleagues. Teachers are well placed – in many cases best placed – to understand the organisational dynamics of their own schools and to use this understanding to inform their own strategic action for change and improvement, but such wisdom needs to be cultivated and developed through a programme of support.

In order that teachers might embrace the idea of leadership they need opportunities to experience it and to learn from that experience through systematic reflection.

The task of leadership may seem especially daunting for those who have little positional power and authority in the organisation.

Perhaps the most important proposal here is that teachers should be encouraged to think about the task as having the three dimensions set out in the diagram above:

It is the strategic approach in which all three are integrated – or at least in harmony with each other – that will lead to successful improvements in teaching and learning and the long-term building of capacity.

Supporting the activity

Here the activity is actually leading development work rather than preparing for it or planning it. External supporters and programme or group leaders need to concentrate on what has to be done to provide teachers with ongoing support for what is undoubtedly a very difficult job. Part D contains a considerable amount of information with which you should become familiar. This section contains additional guidance organised under the following headings:

- Embracing leadership
- Managing the discourse
- Focusing on collaboration
- Focusing on experimenting with practice
- Focusing on gathering and using evidence
- Focusing on impact

(a) Embracing leadership

Many teachers will find the idea of exercising leadership daunting. The 'Clarifying values and concerns' exercise (Workshop 4, p. 76) should help to build confidence, but this has to be reinforced and developed as often as possible. Within group sessions you need to provide opportunities for participants to consider arguments in support of teacher leadership. Michael Fullan's argument about education as a moral enterprise and the responsibility on the part of all teachers to lead and manage change may be useful here (Fullan 1993). The headings in Resource 32 (p. 127) can be used to structure discussion.

Although being committed to the leadership enterprise is necessary, it is not sufficient. Most teachers will find that taking on leadership involves a steep learning curve so they need to be able to explore what kind of tasks and roles leadership involves. Workshop 8 (p. 83) uses statements on cards (Resource 33, p. 128) to enable participants to explore leadership tasks by sorting and prioritising. The exercise also allows teachers to reflect on their natural style and to consider the values that underpin the way they might approach the leadership of development work.

(b) Managing the discourse

Teachers need to learn about leadership by engaging in authentic and honest reflection on the concrete experience of their attempts to lead development work. Programme providers and group leaders need to work continuously to create and maintain the conditions that allow this to happen. Our research tells us that teachers' capacity for reflection is often constrained by the micro-political tensions that are normally manifest in most of the meetings they attend, but their support group led by an external consultant or university tutor tends to be relatively free of this constraint. In Part B it is suggested that an ethical code of practice be adopted to provide a safe environment within which teachers can openly discuss the hazards and pitfalls of managing change (see Resource 4, p. 97). This should not be treated as a one-off event; the principles of what Habermas calls 'the ideal speech situation' (White 1988) have to be returned to, and the observation of these principles has to be regarded as the responsibility of all participants.

The environment for discussion about leading development work is not just a matter of such issues as confidentiality; it also has to be experienced as positively supportive so that participants feel that it is rewarding to open up their experience to the scrutiny of their fellow group members. This means that group leaders have to cultivate a supportive climate that involves working on the quality of relationships within the group, building trust and a sense of friendship. It is also a matter of being flexible to allow the programme to be adjusted to take account of events and emotions that arise. The vignette in Figure E1 below illustrates this.

It was 4.35 pm and the meeting of the school-based development group had just begun. The university tutor leading the session had just reminded everybody of the agenda for that session, which was to include a seminar about spirituality and collective worship, since these were issues that featured in the development work of at least two group members. There was also to be a workshop activity designed to help participants think through their strategies for running staff development events. Just as the university tutor had finished outlining the agenda, someone arrived late and in an emotional state. Martha was the acting head of technology. She apologised for the lateness and the interruption and said that she would not be able to stay long because she had to go home to prepare something for the next day. Her colleagues could see that she was upset and so asked what had happened. Martha explained to the group that she had just come from the head teacher's office where she had 'been given a rough ride' by the head and a member of the governing body about her plans for the development of the new technology building. She had been told that her ideas were unworkable and the costs of various elements of the refurbishment not clear. She was asked to prepare a proper business plan and present it to the head at 8.00 am the next morning. The group responded sympathetically and it was suggested that the planned agenda could be set aside so that Martha could rehearse her business plan with her colleagues. The discussion lasted for over an hour and drew upon the collective wisdom of the ten or so members of the group. They enabled Martha to become clear about what her plan needed to say and they challenged her when her thinking was woolly or not sufficiently strategic. Martha thanked the group for helping her through this crisis and they all agreed that the exercise had been instructive. The next morning Martha presented her new plan to the head teacher who was said to be both surprised and impressed.

Figure E1 Emphasising support

The vignette describes a rather dramatic event but it brings into sharp focus an important function of the group as a source of support for those attempting to lead development work. Group leaders need to provide, on a regular basis, structured opportunities for reflecting on the experience of leading change. This should not be left to chance or assumed to be taking place in the informal exchanges that accompany the meetings of the group or network. Group meetings should include pair work and small group discussions supported with prompt questions or formats to ensure that all group members have sufficient opportunities to talk about their experience of leading change, and to gain the benefits of critical feedback from their colleagues. The group leaders should take every opportunity to highlight the interrelation of the three dimensions of the process:

- managing change through collaboration;
- experimenting with practice;
- gathering and using evidence.

Each of these is discussed below.

(c) Focusing on collaboration

Group leaders should draw upon Workshop 9 (p. 85) to enable participants to explore the concept of organisational culture and strategies for analysing the school's culture. If the school as a whole has used self-evaluation tools or instruments for analysing the culture, these activities can be usefully discussed. The material in Part D ('Leading development work', pp. 39–48) can also be used to explore a range of strategies for engaging in collaborative development work. It is important to take every opportunity to make the links between this discussion and the 'experimenting with practice' and 'gathering and using evidence' dimensions. Group leaders also need to make a link between these discussions and planning for impact, for example, using Resources 27 (p. 122) and 39 (p. 134).

(d) Focusing on experimenting with practice

It is argued that teachers in the UK are particularly shy of looking at each other's teaching or professional practice more generally. Group leaders can encourage participants to embrace experimenting with practice by emphasising the need to evaluate ideas and proposals in action. Case study material such as Julie's story (Resource 41, p. 136) or Richard's story (Resource 42, p. 137) can be used to highlight the way development work can build on such classroom-focused work. The material in Part D (see pp. 42–4 and Figure D11) can be used as the basis for discussion and planning activities. It is important to ensure that there are regular opportunities for participants to relate stories about such experiments within the group programme in order to sharpen their perspectives and draw others into the enterprise. Again, the links between these discussions and the other two dimensions should not be neglected otherwise teachers may be tempted to focus solely on their own classrooms in such a way as to restrict knowledge creation and wider transfer.

(e) Focusing on gathering and using evidence

The vision of evidence-based practice espoused by Hargreaves (1996) and others has to be nurtured by ongoing support for the values of systematic inquiry. There may well be some excellent guidance at the point of planning, but the extent to which teachers actually develop practical wisdom about how to gather and use evidence is most likely to be gained through ongoing reflection on their experience of attempting it. Workshop 10 (p. 88) can be used to frame this discussion, but group leaders need to return to these issues on a regular basis and be responsive to the growing level of awareness. The issues discussed in Part D under the headings of 'rigour', 'ethics', 'analysis' and 'interpretation' (pp. 46–7) need to be addressed through discussion of real cases. The overarching issue of adopting a strategic approach to inquiry should be highlighted in making the links between the three dimensions of leading development work.

(f) Focusing on impact

At the end of the section 'Leading development work' (Part D, pp. 39–48), the guidance focuses on the outcomes of the development work. In Workshop 11 (p. 90), teachers are urged to reflect on the impact of their work by using Resources 39 and 40 (pp. 134–5). The writing of the critical narrative is a key vehicle for thinking through the range of outcomes, some of which will be unanticipated and unexpected. This means that group leaders should allow time within the programme to work on the idea of the critical narrative. Again this should not be a one-off discussion – the art of constructing a narrative that makes sense of the experience and challenges our thinking needs to be cultivated through numerous opportunities to relate experiences of the development work within the safe but critical environment of the group. Wisdom about the possible impact of development work is thus developed over time and then informs future planning.

Presentation and accreditation

Evidence of development work and reflection on the process should be retained so that a selection can be made to include in the portfolio.

Transforming professional knowledge

This is the final stage of the process of teacher-led development work. Group leaders will need to be familiar with the section 'Transforming professional knowledge' in Part D (pp. 48–50).

Rationale

We tend to think of learning as being something that happens to individuals, but of course organisations too can learn (Senge 1990; Argyris and Schon 1996). In order for schools to develop cohesion and a strong 'collective vision', the institutional memory needs to be nourished so that the knowledge gained through development work is retained and built upon. The interests and priorities of individual teachers may change – they may take on different responsibilities or move to another school – and in this event the school can still build on its capacity for improvement if the knowledge has been successfully shared.

As already mentioned, schools are data-rich institutions and we have discussed in 'Documenting the process' (above) the need for systematic documentation, but it is not enough to stockpile data and evidence year after year. What needs to be cultivated is the practical wisdom about improvement that requires collective engagement with evidence. This is a process that feeds into long-term school improvement, building on successes and learning from mistakes in the ever-changing context.

Accounts of teachers' development work can easily be consigned to a filing cabinet instead of providing important resources for the school. The profession as a whole should be drawing on this knowledge through networks with other schools and wider professional bodies as well as through collaborative activities. This requires thinking beyond the idea of dissemination. The 'hopeful scattering' approach is inadequate – we need instead to move towards a model that encourages collective learning and ongoing support for the *transformation* of ideas and knowledge into other contexts. This is complex and requires time and support within collaborative cultures (see 'Leading development work', above). David Hargreaves's (1999a) writing is most illuminating and challenging in this area while Andy Hargreaves and colleagues write realistically about developing supportive cultures (Hargreaves *et al.* 2001).

Supporting the activity

In Part D (pp. 40–2; 48–50), we discussed how teachers' development work can draw colleagues into the experiment and spread the knowledge through a range of collaborative activities. The support group is also a good forum for knowledge-sharing and fostering collaboration. Indeed, such a group can form a critical mass in the school, spreading innovation and transforming the organisational culture.

If participants are registered for a Masters degree or other postgraduate academic award, the process of supervision, submission of written work and its assessment should make a major contribution to the quality of the professional knowledge encapsulated in that work. The academic process should ensure a high degree of rigour, considerable clarity about what has been gained, an effective synthesis of that knowledge and a reliable evaluation of the strength of the claims that can be made about particular professional practices. However, there is a major difficulty in that, traditionally, the award-bearing context has tended to lead to a situation in which the university is the sole audience for the teachers' accounts of their development work. We suggest that there is a great deal more that university partners can do to facilitate the dissemination of the knowledge that arises from teachers' development work.

First, group leaders can encourage participants to plan their writing and presentation for multiple purposes, adapting materials from a portfolio or dissertation to produce accounts in different formats for a variety of different audiences. This is an affirming process and will encourage them and develop confidence in making the most of what they are learning through their leadership of development work.

Partners, programme providers and group leaders should discuss how effectively teachers' accounts are being used within the participants' schools. Ultimately, knowledge management is the responsibility of the head teacher or principal, but it may be that the partnership can offer support.

Beyond this, the programme should be able to facilitate the articulation of the teacher's voice by providing support for the publication of accounts of development work as set out in Figure E2 below.

> in a network journal or magazine
>
> on the network web site
>
> on linked web sites
>
> through participation in online discussion activities
>
> in the form of presentations at conferences
>
> as papers in professional and research journals
>
> as chapters in edited books
>
> through membership of consultative policy formation groups
>
> through collaborations with teachers in other schools

Figure E2 Publishing accounts of teachers' development work

As we suggest in Part B, partners can build a network that provides the infrastructure for support for publication of this sort. Leadership of development work should result in a range of presentations and publications for different audiences and purposes. Initiatives such as the Best Practice Research Scholarship scheme (Department for Education and Skills) and the Networked Learning Communities programme in England can provide additional funding and frameworks to support this endeavour.

In our experience, this kind of activity is highly valued by teachers and enables them both to locate their work and understanding in the wider discourse and to build on it through learning from colleagues. Over time, an informal network of individual contacts and links will be developed within any formal structure as teachers find colleagues who share the same values and professional interests. This should be fostered by ensuring that network conferences allow sufficient time and space for such links to be made and reinforced.

Presentation and accreditation

Partners need to keep under review the question of whether the presentation of portfolios and dissertations for the purposes of an academic award is assisting the process of knowledge creation or hindering it. In Part B we suggested that the university should review its accreditation framework. This needs to be revisited at regular intervals to ensure that the requirements – or what might be perceived to be the requirements – of the academic process are in fact supporting teachers in making the best possible contribution, not only to the improvement of teaching and learning in their schools but also to the expansion and broadening of professional knowledge.

Part F

Workshops

This section contains a series of workshops to support groups of teachers leading development work. Each workshop focuses on an element of the process and is headed to correspond with the parallel sections in Parts C, D and E of the book, as listed below.

Introduction
    1   Introducing the process of teacher-led development work

Critical reflection
    2   Developing a critical approach to practice

Documenting the process
    3   Portfolio review

Clarifying values and concerns
    4   Reflecting on values and concerns

Personal development planning
    5   Identifying personal development priorities
    6   Planning development work to maximise impact

Strategic action planning
    7   Strategic action planning

Leading development work
    8   Leading development work
    9   Analysing school cultures and engaging in collaboration
   10   Practical inquiry to support development work

Transforming professional knowledge
   11   Making a difference: widening the impact of development work

As explained in Part E, these workshops and activities are intended to be illustrative of support for teacher-led development work that can be provided through school- or area-based groups. This part of the book is *not* intended to provide a 'course' in its entirety. Group leaders should select and adapt these materials as appropriate and will need to add many other activities, following the principles and guidelines in Part E, to meet individual needs and to fit the particular context.

Workshop 1 Introducing the process of teacher-led development work

This workshop is intended to be used as an introduction for teachers who have expressed an interest or who are already committed to a programme or scheme to support their leadership of development work. It is best led jointly by representatives of the supporting partnership as explained in Part E ('Introducing the support framework', pp. 51–2). Workshop leaders should make themselves fully familiar with the ideas outlined in Parts A, B and C of the book before introducing them to a group of teachers. They should also read 'Introducing the support framework' section (see above) in preparation.

Purpose of the workshop

• To introduce the ideas and argument behind this approach, in particular the concepts of human agency and capacity to make a difference.
• To present the framework to support teacher-led development work and to introduce some of its characteristics.
• To allow participants to relate this to their own current experience, raise issues of concern and contribute to the early planning and discussion about the way in which the group will work.

Resources needed

• Overhead projector transparencies of the following:
  Resource 5   A framework for teacher-led development work (diagram)
  Resource 6   Leading development work (diagram)
  Resource 25 Planning for impact (headings)
• Photocopies of Resource 4 Ethical principles for a support group (example).
• Sticky labels or cards with adhesive to mount on the wall or board, large enough to be visible to the whole group.
• Marker pens.

Introducing the activity

Workshop leaders should plan an introductory presentation to explain this approach to school improvement which rests on the belief that teachers can make a real difference within their own professional situations, and contribute to school improvement and wider professional learning. Partners should each be given the opportunity to express their conviction and commitment to this purpose. Participants will need to know what the particular programme or scheme entails, how the group will operate and how it will be supported by partnership arrangements, but do make sure that the key ideas about agency and school improvement are not obscured by the practical details.

Workshop leaders should use the first three resources (Resources 5, 6 and 25) on a projector or as handouts to explain the approach in their own context. Parts A, B and C of the book should be used to plan this introductory presentation.

Introduce the idea that a support group needs to have ethical principles governing its activities and discussions (this is discussed fully in Part B). The example (Resource 4) illustrates the kinds of principles that might be appropriate.

The activity

Ask participants to form groups of three or four and to discuss what they have heard so far. Distribute the cards or labels and marker pens and ask them to:

(a) take turns to explain briefly what they hope to get out of involvement in the group;

(b) write down clearly the key issues that have emerged as the presentation was made. These may be practical ('will we have time?') or philosophical (the concept of teacher leadership may be alien). They do not all have to be problems – encourage both positive and questioning responses. Workshop leaders may like to circulate during this time to support the discussion.

Debriefing

Ask the groups in turn to offer their key issues and combine all responses on a board or on the wall to represent the different aspects of concern/reaction. Workshop leaders should then respond with explanations or open up the discussion to the whole group as appropriate. The presence of representatives of the partnership will enable responses from different perspectives and ensure that all the participants are aware of the issues being raised in these initial stages.

Follow-up

It would be useful to record the discussion and the points made, and type this up to circulate back to participants. The ethical principles for the group should be discussed once the membership of the group has been established, and again typed up and circulated.

As explained in 'Introducing the support framework' (Part E), the priorities for the initial stages are to ensure that the practical arrangements and coordination of the programme or scheme are running smoothly, and in particular that dates and times of meetings and contact details are circulated. It is recommended that frequent review and planning meetings are held between supporting partners while the group is being established.

Workshop 2   Developing a critical approach to practice

This workshop is to support critical reflection in the early stages once participants have started to lead development work. First read the 'Critical reflection' sections in Parts D and E.

Purpose of the workshop

- To encourage teachers to reflect more systematically on their everyday practice.
- To build confidence in talking and writing about experience and practice.
- To develop a more critical approach in thinking about practice.

Resources needed

- You need to prepare copies of:
      Resource 9   Exploring the issues in classroom practice
      Resource 10 A critical incident in classroom practice
      Resource 11 Two narratives
      Resource 12 How to make writing critical
- A flipchart or whiteboard may be useful at the end.

Introducing the activity

Explain the purposes of the workshop as listed above but do not spend too long on preparation as this may reduce the spontaneity of the exercise. You may wish to refer to reflective exercises already completed, e.g. the initial statement, and explain that the workshop helps to show how the reflection already embedded in everyday practice can be deepened through adopting a critical perspective. The workshop also demonstrates how this can be strengthened through writing.

The activity

Organise group members so that they are quite well spaced and distribute Resource 9. Allow about 20 minutes for them to write about a classroom incident or episode that has occurred in the course of the week (preferably that day). This could be a simple conversation or interaction – something interesting, annoying, inspiring, thought-provoking or typical. There may be a need for considerable reassurance, but remind them that they simply need to tell a story and that a polished piece of writing is not expected.

  If anyone is reticent you may like to use Resource 10 which provides an example of such a piece of writing and show how it is going to be used. (This can be distributed at the end for reference if it is not used at this point.) You can also pick up on points that have arisen in conversation as incidents to write about or give prompts, e.g. ask them to describe something positive that has happened during their day or something about which they are concerned.

  Once the writing is complete, work in pairs to tell each story in turn and then work through the questions. Encourage the 'listeners' to think of questions that will help to explore the issues arising from the stories.

Debriefing

Collect together the *issues* that have emerged through the exploration of these incidents. There is no need for stories to be shared with the whole group – although this is usually fascinating if it does happen. Through questioning and discussion using the mirror of everyone's experience, the consideration of these issues will become more critical. This will be even more powerful where there is common ground and may highlight themes that the group will find helpful to explore in more depth in a future session with the support of some literature.

Participants may also like to discuss how they felt about writing their stories down and the extent to which they found this exercise valuable.

Follow-up

This technique of telling a story and then questioning can be applied to any writing. The specific use of critical incident analysis can be applied to events and episodes during the development process. Reading should be recommended to reinforce this (Tripp 1993; Skoyles *et al.* 1998) particularly if it becomes a major part of the inquiry process. For example, development work focusing on behaviour management or inclusion may need to address the issues through a series of incidents that give particular cause for concern.

Workshop 3   Portfolio review

This workshop can be used once the development work is well underway and evidence has been collected. Workshop leaders should read the sections on 'Documenting the process' in Parts D and E.

Purpose of the workshop

• To reinforce the purposes and format of portfolios of evidence of teacher-led development work.
• Participants to review their portfolios of evidence and commentary, and plan any further work required to improve them.

Resources needed

• Overhead transparencies and/or handouts:
    Resource 13 Examples of evidence in a portfolio
    Resource 15 Uses of a portfolio
    Resource 16 Principles for portfolio construction
• Copies of:
    Resource 17 Portfolio review. Workshop leaders may want to adapt this to their local circumstances, taking into account the professional requirements within schools and where relevant the assessment criteria, presentation protocols and academic conventions of the relevant accrediting body.
• If necessary, copies of:
    Resource 18 From portfolio to dissertation
• Examples of completed portfolios of teacher-led development work where available.
• Participants should be asked to bring any materials relating to their development work that they may include in their portfolios. This may be fully organised in a neat file or several files with different labels, or simply a box full of unsorted papers. Participants should be reassured that the workshop will help them to make sense of this material, therefore it is important to bring it to the session even if it appears chaotic.

Introducing the activity

Workshop leaders should use the overheads and/or handouts (Resources 13, 15 and 16) to remind participants about the evidence that can be included in portfolios, the different purposes of constructing portfolios and the basic principles. Various questions may be raised which should be answered as far as possible before the activity begins.

The activity

Distribute Resource 17 and arrange the group into pairs. Participants should review their portfolios or collections of material by taking turns to talk through their material with partners, using the guide sheet as a prompt. Action points can be recorded by the person listening and handed over at the end.

Debriefing

Any issues that were raised in paired discussion can be discussed with the whole group.

It would be appropriate at this point to give any specific instructions and guidance relating to submission for accreditation where this is relevant. Participants will need to know details of assessment criteria and conventions for presentation. Where submission for accreditation takes the form of a dissertation, spend some time working with Resource 18, which shows how a portfolio relates to a dissertation. Examples of completed portfolios may be handed round, but ensure that participants are aware of the extent to which they have freedom to present their work in their own style.

Follow-up

Ensure that participants receive sufficient individual guidance in the compilation of their portfolios including support and feedback on critical writing.

Refer back to the portfolios as working documents supporting leadership of change, and encourage individuals to adapt the materials for different audiences and different purposes.

Within partnerships supporting teacher-led development work discuss how the portfolios, or selected information extracted from them, may contribute to the institutional archive. Issues of ownership will need to be discussed within schools and with individual participants.

Workshop 4   Reflecting on values and concerns

This workshop is to support the first stage of the model. Workshop leaders should first read the 'Clarifying values and concerns' sections in Parts D and E.

Purpose of the workshop

- To support participants in beginning the process of systematic reflection.
- To provide 'scaffolding' for reflecting on values and concerns as a preparation for the identification of personal development priorities.
- To prepare participants for writing an initial statement.

Resources needed

- Workshop leaders will need to prepare copies of:
    Resource 19 Clarifying values and concerns (discussion sheet)
    Resource 20 Clarifying values and concerns (guide sheet)
    Resource 21 Initial statement (example)

Introducing the activity

Workshop leaders should initiate a discussion about the relationship between individual teachers' development priorities and those of the school as an organisation. Michael Fullan's argument about the moral purpose of teaching and the role of the teacher as an agent of change may be useful here (Fullan 1993, 1999 and 2001). It is important to emphasise aspects of the argument outlined in Part A of this book to highlight that the effectiveness of improvement strategies depends on individuals' development priorities arising out of their values and concerns, rather than simply imposed or dictated either by external agencies or senior colleagues or groups within the management hierarchy of the school.

The activity

Organise group members into pairs in a space large enough to allow for sufficient privacy and distribute copies of Resource 19. Participants should then be asked to interview each other in turn using headings and prompt questions on the guide sheet. The interviewer can use Resource 20 to make notes that can be handed over to the interviewee at the end of the workshop.

It is important to allow at least half an hour for each interview.

The activity can also be carried out in trios. A can interview B while C takes detailed notes. This has the advantage of allowing the interviewer to concentrate on asking the questions and lessens the inhibiting effect of the note-taking. It is also likely to result in improved note-taking. The disadvantages are that it may be slightly less intimate and will take a little more time.

Debriefing

Participants should be asked to comment on any areas of difficulty and concepts such as 'professional values' should be clarified. This may also present an opportunity to discuss any general issues, for example, any lack of clarity or scepticism about organisational matters such as 'consultation'.

Follow-up

Participants should be encouraged to draft an initial statement as soon as possible after the workshop using the notes taken by their partner in the interview activity. Resource 21 can be used to illustrate the kind of document and language required.

Workshop 5   Identifying personal development priorities

This workshop enables participants to work on the ideas arising from their reflections in order to shape some proposals for change. They therefore need to have clarified their professional values and concerns. The workshop will be most successful when this has been formalised through the writing of an initial statement (see 'Clarifying values and concerns' in Part D). Plans are developed individually and then discussed with key people and groups in the school to ensure that the focus and scope of the plans are appropriate and realistic. Workshop leaders should first read the sections on 'Personal development planning' in Parts D and E.

Purpose of the workshop

- To enable participants to draw together their initial ideas about development priorities.
- To facilitate understanding of the format and function of a personal development plan.
- To discuss how to negotiate the plan within the school to ensure it is linked to the school development plan.

Resources needed

- Copies of:
     Resource 23 Personal development plan (example)
     Resource 24 Personal development plan (guide sheet)
- Flipchart or whiteboard.
- Participants may be asked to bring with them their initial statements and any other relevant documentation, e.g. notes on discussions about their role and responsibilities within the school.

Introducing the activity

Workshop leaders should ensure that all participants are clear about the difference between development work and maintenance, and that this workshop has a development focus. This will provide another opportunity to reinforce the idea of individuals as 'change agents' as a key strategy for school improvement (see Fullan 1993).

A good way to do this is to ask participants to recall activities in which they have been involved during the day (or the agenda of the last meeting they attended) and write them on the board or flipchart. Then identify from the jumble on the board those concerned with maintenance and those concerned with development. This may prompt considerable discussion about how time is used, particularly in meetings; you may decide as a group to return to this theme in a future session.

The activities

1 Whole-group discussion of personal development plans

Distribute the example of a personal development plan (Resource 23) or another similar example. Allow time to read it through, then discuss the nature of the document:

- it is brief (no more than one page);
- it clarifies development priorities in the context of individual roles and responsibilities and relevant school development initiatives;

- it is for a professional rather than an academic audience;
- it is not a private document but a public statement to be used as the basis for discussion with people within the school.

2 Trios for identifying personal development priorities

Participants should work in threes to enable sufficient individual focus but at the same time allow a challenging discussion. One person will give a personal account, one will help to develop ideas by asking questions and the third will write notes to be handed afterwards to the person giving the account. These roles should be circulated, dividing the time available to allow everyone a chance to discuss their focus.

Members of the trio should give a brief verbal summary of their role(s), responsibilities and concerns leading to exploration of personal development priorities. The notes from this discussion should be written as far as possible under the headings on Resource 24 so that they can be used to support the drafting of personal development plans.

Debriefing

The following issues should be drawn out:

- the importance of being realistic about development plans in terms of what the individual can achieve and also what can be achieved in the particular school context;
- the potential conflict between individual priorities, values and aspirations and the school development agenda;
- the importance of negotiation and consultation with appropriate people and groups with the school (this will include colleagues but may also involve pupils, parents, governors, external advisors and people in the wider community).

Follow-up

Participants should be asked to draft a personal development plan, clarify who needs to be consulted, conduct the necessary discussions and redraft the personal development plan accordingly.

At this point tutors may wish to negotiate a date by which the plans will be completed and handed in to provide the basis for tutorial discussions with individuals.

The completed plan should be included in the portfolio of development work and will be helpful when reviewing progress.

Workshop 6 Planning development work to maximise impact

This workshop supports teachers in thinking about the possible effects of their development work. Development work is likely to have greater impact if, at the planning stage, consideration is given to the full range of possible outcomes. This is part of the personal development planning process and should help teachers to refine their development plans. Workshop leaders should first read the 'Personal development planning' sections in Parts D and E.

In the planning of development work it is important to try to predict the impact on pupils, teachers, the school as an organisation and other schools.

Purpose of the workshop

- To provide a framework for teachers to consider the possible outcomes of their development work.
- To help teachers to focus on detail and consider the wider implications of their development work.
- To provide a basis for planning to maximise impact.

Resources needed

- Overhead transparency or handout:
    Resource 25 Planning for impact (headings)
- Copies of:
    Resource 26 A case study of a teacher's development work: Alison's story
    Resource 27 Planning for impact (guide sheet)
- Participants should bring copies of their personal development plans, whether written up formally or in note or draft form.

Introducing the activity

Begin the session by asking everyone to state briefly their focus for development. Concentrate on the changes in practice that they intend to introduce; inquiry should be seen as supporting these changes.

Explain the purpose of the workshop and introduce the different dimensions of impact that participants can consider using the OHT (Resource 25). Take some time to work through this and consider the possibilities, extending and intensifying thinking about development plans by exploring individuals' situations and ideas to draw everyone into the discussion.

If participants do not feel confident – particularly about the ways in which they might effect change beyond their individual classrooms – you may like to use the case study (Resource 26) to extend thinking about how the development work might have implications for colleagues, pupils and other schools. Participants may find it useful to identify the impact of this teacher's work under the headings in Resource 25.

The activity

Distribute Resource 27 and ask participants to work individually to consider their own development work under the headings and prompts. This is a detailed exercise but individuals will concentrate on different aspects of impact depending on their focus, their role within the school, the context within which they are working and so on. The tutor should move around the room to offer support and ideas but participants could also share their ideas in pairs and support one another's thinking.

Debriefing

Allow 10–15 minutes at the end of the session for feedback that may have implications for the group, the school and supporting network. For example, the group might benefit from a session to consider particular aspects of pupils' learning to support, schools may need to consider the opportunities for collaboration in order to maximise professional learning and ideas may emerge about how to share between schools.

Follow-up

The planning sheet should be included in the development portfolio where it can be used as the basis for review of progress and a reminder of the different aspects of impact that the development work might address. It can be considered as a 'statement of intention'; it is likely that opportunities and changing circumstances may require it to be modified.

The planning sheet can also be used in discussions with colleagues within the school to ensure that the development work receives support to enable individuals to maximise impact, e.g. it may prompt the setting of dates for sharing the work in progress or to report on a completed project, and it can reinforce and make explicit the links between the development work and different aspects of the school development plan.

Workshop 7   Strategic action planning

This workshop enables participants to break down the development plan into manageable practical sections that will make change happen. Workshop leaders should read the sections 'Strategic action planning' in Parts D and E.

Purpose of the workshop

- To enable participants to develop action plans to address the agreed personal development priorities.
- To encourage participants to plan strategically to maximise the impact of their work.

Resources needed

- Copies of:
  Resource 13 Examples of evidence in a portfolio – if needed
  Resource 28 Strategic action planning: considering the obstacles and opportunities
  Resource 29 Action plan (example)
  Resource 30 Sample development priorities
  Resource 31 Action plan (guide sheet)
- Overhead transparency:
  Resource 6   Leading development work (diagram)
- Participants should bring copies of their personal development plans to the session.

Introducing the activities

First, workshop leaders should emphasise the purpose of written action plans:

- to ensure that development work is planned and systematic;
- to ensure that intentions are discussed with colleagues;
- to ensure that the development work is strategic;
- to ensure rigour in evidence gathering;
- to facilitate critical feedback with a view to maximising the effectiveness of the action to be taken.

It is important to achieve a balance between the three dimensions of leading development work expressed in the diagram. These are:

(a)   managing change through collaboration
(b)   experimenting with practice
(c)   gathering and using evidence.

The activities

1 Whole-group discussion of the action plan facsimile

Use the action plan example (Resource 29) to explore the nature of action plans for development work. Emphasise the way in which the writer has chosen headings that fit her purpose – influenced but not constrained by the guidance headings. Point out the elements of collaborating to manage change, gathering and using evidence, and experimenting with practice that comprise leadership of development work, using Resource 6 as a reminder. Explain the relationship between the longer-term personal development plan and the short-term action plans.

2 Small group task: devising action plans

Now ask participants to work in groups of three or four. Give out one of the development priorities (Resource 30) to each group (or devise development priorities relevant to the school and context) and ask them to consider what they would write under each of the headings of the action plan format (Resource 27) and to appoint a spokesperson.

Allow at least 20 minutes for the group discussion. Ask the spokesperson from each group to read out the sample development plan and then to summarise the group's agreed action plan.

Debriefing

In the discussion following this exercise the workshop leader should try to draw out issues such as:

- strategies for collaborating with colleagues to achieve lasting improvements;
- the practicalities of conducting inquiry that is realistic within the constraints of time and other resources;
- the cyclical nature of action and inquiry and the vital role of critical reflection in development work (refer back to the 'Critical reflection' sections in Parts D and E).

If group members have no experience of data gathering or inquiry strategies the workshop leaders may wish to offer a checklist such as Resource 13.

Follow-up

Participants should be asked to draft at least one action plan either at the end of the session or immediately afterwards. These may be collected and critical feedback offered. It must be stressed that the action plans have to be seen as published documents to be shown to colleagues within the school to secure their agreement and cooperation. If there is significant objection to an action plan, this indicates that the development work will be problematic and needs to be reviewed.

Participants should be encouraged to read about the role of inquiry in development work; the literature on action research is useful here and some of the literature on school improvement may also be helpful.

Workshop 8   Leading development work

This is the first in a series of workshops that support the leadership of development work. Here the activity and discussion focuses on the role of leaders or change agents in school development work, through encouraging participants to reflect on their own experiences of school change. Workshop leaders should first read the sections on 'Leading development work' in Parts D and E.

Purpose of the workshop

- To enable participants to reflect on issues arising from their experience as practitioners involved in change.
- To explore the nature of the role of leaders of school change.

Resources needed

- Handouts or overhead transparency:
    Resource 32 Role of the change agent (headings)
- Set of cards:
    Resource 33 Leadership tasks (labels for cards). These should be enlarged and stuck onto cards (postcard size is ideal). Make extra sets of cards if you have a larger group – it is best to divide into sub-groups of about six people.

Introducing the activity

It is assumed that participants will already have framed action plans and will be taking steps to implement them. Everyone will have had previous experience of managing change and of 'being managed'.

First, the workshop leader will need to provide a framework for the activity. Michael Fullan's (1993) discussion about the moral purpose of education and the four dimensions of the role of change agent (personal vision building, inquiry, mastery and collaboration) is an effective text for thinking about the responsibility that all of us have as agents of change, and to explore the conviction that teachers are key agents of school change. The OHT or handout (Resource 32) shows these headings. Further literature on teacher leadership and agency can be recommended to participants.

Some teachers may be uncomfortable or totally unfamiliar with the concept of being a change agent, in which case it may be useful to share some experiences of implementing, managing and leading change to demonstrate that this is part of normal professional practice.

The activity

This is a card-sorting activity prepared from Resource 33. Each card carries a statement describing a function of the change agent. The group(s) should be asked to sort and evaluate the cards. This can be done in a number of ways but two suggestions are given here.

(a) Put the cards in a single pile, face downwards. Each person in turn picks up the top card and comments on it: whether they would do this, whether it is a good strategy for supporting change, and so on. Other members of the group may wish to add comments. The group may then place the card in an 'accept' or 'reject' pile. Once all the cards have been discussed and sorted, the group can then look at the accepted cards and try to agree on a statement that sums up their values and views about managing change. If there are several groups, these statements can be shared and discussed at the end.

(b)   Place the cards face upwards on a table and ask the group to arrange them in a shape that represents their values and views about leading and managing change. The search for consensus will lead to a discussion about the value of different strategies. When completed, a spokesperson for the group should explain the pattern to the group leader and, if appropriate, to the other groups.

Debriefing

The workshop leader should draw out the tensions in the change agent's role, for example the question of the balance between leadership based on expertise and the need for facilitation to encourage ownership and collegiality. It is likely that issues will be raised about implementing school reform that is imposed through policy and change that 'grows' from within.

Follow-up

Participants should be encouraged to read about school change. It may be useful to seek volunteers from the discussion groups to type up the agreed statements or summarise the discussion so that they can compare their experiences and ideas with the ideas in the literature.

The need to consult fully about action plans should be stressed again, in particular the importance of discussing with senior colleagues the management issues arising.

Workshop 9   Analysing school cultures and engaging in collaboration

The school culture has an enormous influence on the process and impact of teacher-led development work. It is therefore vital that teachers understand the existing culture to enable them to work effectively within it. They may also seek to contribute to the shaping of the culture in order to make it more conducive to change and to the building of organisational capacity. Workshop leaders should read in preparation the sections on 'Collaborating to manage change' in Parts D and E.

The activities here can be used together in one session or divided up and used in separate sessions as required.

Purpose of the workshop

- To raise participants' awareness of the complex cultures of schools.
- To provide conceptual frameworks for analysing the culture within which they are leading change.
- To provide an opportunity to consider the network of communications and pattern of consultation and collaboration that will best support the change process.

Resources needed

- For activity 1, copies of:
    Resource 34 Descriptions of school cultures. You may also wish to find a few brief definitions of school culture from the literature or use other sources as suggested in Part E.
- For activity 2, copies of:
    Resource 35 Engaging with the school as an organisation (copied to provide one 'incident' per sheet).

Introducing the activities

This workshop – or elements or versions of it – can be used at different stages of the process of managing change. The activities and discussion should be adapted to meet the needs of members of the group; workshop leaders will need to judge the scope of ideas that can be meaningfully introduced at different times.

Workshop leaders might find it useful to develop their perspective on questions of human agency and social structures beforehand by reading, for example, Giddens (1984) and Mitchell and Sackney (2000). Models of teacher cultures are neatly explored by Andy Hargreaves (1994).

In introducing the workshop, stress that school development work makes no sense at all as a private activity; leaders of development work must regard working with colleagues, other members of the school and people from the wider community as a vital dimension to their work as agents of change.

In order to engage successfully with their schools as organisations, participants need to develop understanding of two aspects of their own institutions. First, they need to know about the structures and management arrangements that will determine who is consulted about what. This is concerned with the established lines of communication, the structure of responsibilities and the etiquette in their particular school. Secondly, they need to know about the culture of the organisation with which they are trying to engage. This is a far more complex aspect to understand and some definitions of school cultures could be offered as a way into the discussion.

Finally participants should be reminded that the boundaries of 'the school' are by no means fixed. Schools are communities involving many groups and individuals as well as teachers and pupils. They operate within, and overlap with, wider educational, social and political systems and communities. It is therefore important to take a wider view of the context for leadership of change.

Having established the importance of developing understanding of school cultures and communities, two activities are offered here. Consider also other materials that can be used to explore these issues such as the excellent workshop by David Hargreaves (1999b).

1 Describing the school culture

Distribute Resource 34 or any other representations of models of school cultures. Brief definitions from the literature could also be shown here on a handout or OHT. Participants should work alone at the start to reflect on their own experience and compare this with the models represented by ticking the characteristics they recognise. This should take five or ten minutes. It should not be assumed that a school culture will fit one of these categories – it is more likely that a school will show signs of a number of different cultural trends.

Participants should then be asked to form twos or threes to compare notes, remembering that individuals' perceptions of their school's culture are likely to vary. It may be necessary to suggest that the discussion should focus on understanding rather than criticism and on 'what can we change?' rather than 'who can we blame?', particularly if participants are working in difficult circumstances.

If the group comprises several teachers from each school, they should then work together to write a description of their school culture, including their own descriptors and titles where appropriate. About 30 minutes should be allowed for this task after which the groups can share their descriptions. If participants are from many different schools they may return to individual working to write their descriptions or feed back into a whole-group discussion. There will be many issues raised through comparison of experiences that can lead to a rich discussion about the nature of the school culture, the factors affecting it and how it might be changed and developed.

2 Strategic planning for engagement

In this activity, participants consider strategies for handling what we might call 'incidents of engagement'. The workshop leaders should organise groups of three or four and hand to each group one scenario from Resource 35. Each group should be asked to discuss possible strategies for engagement to support their leadership of change and then report back to the whole group. The material in the section on 'Managing change through collaboration' in Part D can be used to further explore strategies for collaboration.

Debriefing

For each of the activities, workshop leaders should try to direct discussion towards the practical implications for action and to encourage participants to consider ways of maximising the impact of their development work through effective engagement with individuals, groups and the school as an organisation. This may involve challenging the existing structures and culture of the school and developing new ways of collaborative working. However, there is probably a need to compromise between the adoption of purely pragmatic strategies that will fit within the current system and the development of strategies that are more consistent with the kind of culture that participants would like to see developing with their values. Ethical issues should be raised as problematical and can be discussed further with individuals in tutorials.

Follow-up

Workshop leaders may like to plan future sessions to discuss participants' experiences of engaging with individuals, groups and the institution. The differences between communication, consultation and genuine collaboration could be explored. Participants could share strategies and seek critical feedback from the group.

It may be interesting and valuable for participants to involve others (colleagues, pupils, parents . . .) in analysing the school culture from different perspectives as part of their leadership of change.

Further engagement with the literature should be encouraged.

Workshop 10   Practical inquiry to support development work

This workshop shows how systematic gathering of data and use of evidence can be employed strategically to support teachers' development work. It is assumed that, through previous discussions, participants are already familiar with ideas about data, evidence and inquiry and have been guided towards literature that explains data-gathering strategies and explores methodological issues.

Purpose of the workshop

- To enable participants to consider how to design inquiry that is 'fit for purpose'.
- To show participants how to integrate inquiry with their everyday work.
- To demonstrate the use of evidence as part of a managed change process.

Resources needed

- Overhead transparency:
    Resource 6   Leading development work (diagram)
- Copies of:
    Resource 36 Using evidence
    Resource 37 Strategies for integrating evidence gathering with everyday practice
    Resource 38 Practical inquiry to support development work
- Participants may find it helpful to bring their personal development plans and action plan(s) to the session.

The activity

Use Resource 6 to discuss the way the evidence-gathering dimension of development work is interlinked with the 'managing change through collaboration' and 'experimenting with practice' dimensions.

Using Resource 36, ask participants to consider their purposes and strategies. Resource 38 can be used to talk through the headings, which suggest that teachers need to:

- plan inquiry that is 'fit for purpose';
- use efficient, institution-friendly inquiry strategies;
- integrate inquiry into a managed change process.

Ask participants to work in groups of three or four. For each of the three aspects of practical inquiry, the group should decide on *one* good example from a member of the group and develop it together using the questions on the sheets until the inquiry activity described is as integrated and strategic as possible. Emphasise that the purpose is to think in detail about how inquiry can support the change process, such as ensuring that the data collected yield evidence that is directly relevant and useful, involving pupils, colleagues and others in dialogue around the data, and raising awareness about the development work.

Debriefing

Allow plenty of time for discussion and mutual challenge, then ask groups to report back. Workshop leaders should draw out the issues and develop participants' understanding of the power of inquiry used strategically. It may be important to discuss the following:

- The practicality of different strategies, given the limitations of time, resources etc.
- Integration of inquiry so that there is as little disruption as possible to teaching and learning.
- Appropriateness of strategies chosen, given the types of evidence required.
- Reassurance about the validity of strategies that may not fall within narrow or more traditional definitions of research.
- The importance of giving time to reflect on the meaning of the evidence gathered and to use it as the basis for discussion with colleagues.
- The reciprocal nature of inquiry and development where every activity is seen as an inquiry opportunity and all data can be used to inform the development process.

Follow-up

Group leaders should build in time in future sessions for participants to report back on the way in which they have used inquiry strategically. This might form a theme in their journals and can be picked up in one-to-one discussions with the external critical friend or university tutor.

Participants should be encouraged to use the literature on inquiry and management of change to explore the issues arising from their experiences. Given the obvious time constraints of school-based programmes and activities, the workshop leader could draw attention to selected readings and encourage individuals to report back to the group.

Workshop 11   Making a difference: widening the impact of development work

This workshop is designed for teachers in the later stages of leading development work when inquiry, professional action and reflection have yielded knowledge, ideas and understanding that could be shared with others. It addresses questions of organisational impact and the building of capacity between schools.

Purpose of the workshop

- To enable participants to discuss a range of strategies for transforming professional knowledge through engaging others in the issues and outcomes of development work.
- To widen participants' aspirations and perceptions of their role in contributing to the professional knowledge of individuals, organisations and networks.
- To consider audiences for aspects of their own development work and plan ways of sharing their own professional learning.

Resources needed

- Copies of:
    Resource 41 Reflecting on outcomes: Julie's story
- Handout or overhead transparency:
    Resource 39 Reflecting on the outcomes of your development work
    Resource 40 Reflecting on outcomes (guide sheet)
- Flipchart or whiteboard
- Workshop leaders may wish to ask participants to reflect before the session, see below.

Introducing the activity

Start with a brief summary from each person about where they have reached with their development work and in particular, what they have learnt from it. The checklist in Part D (Figure D7) may help to structure this and prompt participants to think widely about the professional knowledge gained. Workshop leaders may wish to ask participants to prepare for this by reflecting and writing some notes beforehand, but this is not essential.

Explore with the group their own perceptions of the work that they have been leading, and the perceptions that others within the school may have. The work may be seen as a research project with a tenuous link to improving practice or simply a route to further academic qualifications. In either case, portfolios or dissertations are likely to remain on a shelf in the staffroom or at home. Sometimes, however, the work is seen as an integral part of school development and is understood to address school development priorities and contribute to organisational and wider professional learning. In this case, the documentation is a working set of materials and resources that can be used to further disseminate the ideas and understandings.

This may lead into a discussion about the role of teachers in the creation and transmission of professional knowledge. Participants can be asked about how they themselves learn professionally – listening to other teachers, discussion with colleagues and observing and discussing practice elsewhere. Shared learning and the use of both experience and a range of evidence should be highlighted. Having engaged in school-based inquiry and leadership of development work, participants can be proactive in contributing to this professional and organisational learning. This workshop enables participants to consider how they might do this within their own professional situations.

The activity

Organise participants into groups of three or four and hand out the case study (Resource 41) to each person. Ask groups to discuss the example and suggest:

(a) audiences that might benefit from Julie's work;
(b) how Julie might best engage these audiences.

Provide headings (Resource 39) as a prompt. Ask groups also to note issues that emerge in the discussion.

Allow groups five minutes at the end of the discussion to summarise their ideas and the key issues and to appoint a spokesperson.

Briefly draw together ideas about audiences, then note on the flipchart or board the issues raised in the discussion, for example: time, audience response, extent of support within school. Participants may begin to relate these to their own experiences and school contexts.

Finally, ask participants to write notes on the guide sheet (Resource 40) about the ways in which they might take their own development work to wider audiences. After some individual reflection they should take it in turns to talk about their ideas in pairs to develop their ideas.

Debriefing

In the final part of the session, ask participants if there are any ways in which the partnerships supporting their development work, i.e. involving school, university, LEA and/or other agencies, can provide better support in communicating the outcomes and issues arising from their development work. Collect ideas and decide as a group how best to take these forward, taking into account existing structures such as networks and clusters of schools. This should move beyond nominal support and may involve significant challenges and extensions to current practice and the allocation of time and resources.

Follow-up

Dialogue and planning within supporting partnerships should emphasise the value of sharing and learning from development work within and between schools to support individual, collective and organisational learning. Thinking should be steered towards supporting processes, rather than organising events. Celebration of achievement is important but often overlooked or avoided for fear of 'boasting' or making others feel inadequate. It is vital that this is challenged.

Planning sheets filled in at the end of the session can form the basis of individual tutorial discussions. Participants are likely to need considerable individual support to take their ideas forward, especially if their own institutions are not particularly supportive. This may involve feedback on draft reports, practising presentations and activities with a supportive group, moral support through accompanying them to conferences and presentations and so on. They do not have to rely entirely on an external tutor; peer support is equally valuable and should be encouraged as it will lead to further shared learning.

Part G

Resources

This part is a collection of facsimiles, formats, guide sheets, case studies and exemplars that can be photocopied for use by individual teachers and support group leaders.

List of resources

1 Memorandum of agreement (example)
2 Assessment criteria (example)
3 A programme for a support group (example)
4 Ethical principles for a support group (example)
5 A framework for teacher-led development work (diagram)
6 Leading development work (diagram)
7 Outcomes of teacher-led development work (headings)
8 Keeping a journal
9 Exploring the issues in classroom practice
10 A critical incident in classroom practice
11 Two narratives
12 How to make writing critical
13 Examples of evidence in a portfolio
14 Generating documentary evidence
15 Uses of a portfolio
16 Principles for portfolio construction
17 Portfolio review
18 From portfolio to dissertation
19 Clarifying values and concerns (discussion sheet)
20 Clarifying values and concerns (guide sheet)
21 Initial statement (example)
22 Supporting teacher-led development work: key points for head teachers and principals
23 Personal development plan (example)
24 Personal development plan (guide sheet)
25 Planning for impact (headings)
26 A case study of a teacher's development work: Alison's story
27 Planning for impact (guide sheet)
28 Strategic action planning: considering the obstacles and opportunities
29 Action plan (example)
30 Sample development priorities
31 Action plan (guide sheet)
32 Role of the change agent (headings)
33 Leadership tasks (labels for cards)
34 Descriptions of school cultures
35 Engaging with the school as an organisation
36 Using evidence
37 Strategies for integrating evidence gathering with everyday practice
38 Practical inquiry to support development work
39 Reflecting on the outcomes of your development work
40 Reflecting on outcomes (guide sheet)
41 Reflecting on outcomes: Julie's story
42 A case of knowledge transformation: Richard's story

We intend that these resources should be used flexibly by individuals and with groups to support teachers' leadership of development work.

Memorandum of agreement
Muchbinding in the Marsh Comprehensive School

in association with

The University of Pontefract

The following memorandum of agreement sets out the specification of a programme of support for teacher-led development in Muchbinding School.

Aims

The programme will provide support for up to 15 teachers who wish to initiate and lead development work leading to improvements in teaching and learning.

Support staff

The programme will be jointly planned and led by Val Clark, assistant head teacher at the school, and Chris Somers from the university Faculty of Education.

Accreditation

Participants will enrol for the Postgraduate Instructional Leadership Programme which involves progression through Certificate, Diploma and Masters levels. The Certificate and the first part of the Diploma are assessed through the submission of portfolios; the final part of the Diploma requires the submission of a 10,000 word dissertation and the Masters requires the submission of a 20,000 word thesis.

The programme

The support programme will be located at the school except for conferences at the university once each term. There will be at least 12 school-based sessions of 2 hours' duration during the academic year. One-to-one tutorial support will be provided by Chris Somers at the school site, each participant being entitled to at least 3 hours over the course of the academic year.

The specific content of the programme will be planned jointly by Val Clark and Chris Somers in consultation with the group participants and the head teacher, although an overarching theme of 'improving teaching and learning' has been agreed.

Resources

The university will commit at least 15 days of lecturer time at the standard daily rate. In addition to Chris Somers' time, the school will also meet the cost of the registration fee for each participant and will employ a supply teacher for at least one day each term to release participants for one-to-one tutorials. The school staff library will be enhanced to include at least one copy of each item on the list of key texts provided by the Faculty of Education for the Postgraduate Instructional Leadership Programme.

Signed: (Head teacher)

(Director of Postgraduate Programmes, Faculty of Education)

Date:

© David Frost and Judy Durrant 2003

1 Memorandum of agreement (example)

94

Assessment criteria

The criteria set out below are intended to illustrate the kind of criteria that could be used to assess portfolios and dissertations submitted within an award-bearing programme which is supportive of teacher-led development work. Such criteria could be used along-side the university's general criteria for postgraduate work.

Project and planning

Development goals are clarified
Development work is planned and systematic
Development work has been the subject of consultation/negotiation

Use of evidence

Evidence-gathering strategies are appropriate to school-based development work
Inquiry is systematic, well planned and effective
Clear rationale/justification is used for evidence-gathering strategies
Research literature is used to explore methodological issues
Reflection on strategies used demonstrates reflexivity, authenticity and awareness of their limitations

Reflection

Clear and comprehensive account of the development work
Authentic and insightful evaluation of own professional performance and competence
Evidence of awareness of own professional learning
Evidence of review in relation to development goals

Knowledge

Understanding of school development and leadership issues
Understanding of the particular institutional context
Understanding of relevant political, social and policy issues
Knowledge of the literature in relevant fields

Analysis/argument

Issues are located in wider discourse
Literature is used critically
Application of conceptual and analytical frameworks
Testing of theoretical perspectives against experience
Argument is logical and internally consistent
Evidence of evaluation and standpoint-taking

Presentation

Language is used accurately
Material is ordered, labelled and cross-referenced appropriately
Relevant academic protocols have been observed

2 Assessment criteria (example)

St Christopher's School Development Group

Schedule of meetings September–April 2000–2001

A schedule of this kind would be suitable for a group in their second or third year. The initials refer to members of the group who lead parts of the sessions. Each session is arranged for two hours after school.

Date	Focus on development themes	Supporting the development process	Issues raised by the group
Sept. 00	Reporting on current focus and theme (everyone)	Identifying personal development priorities workshop	Guidance on how to spend research funding
Sept. 00	Aspects of pupil motivation (JL, GS)	Action planning workshop	
Oct. 00	Values and the curriculum (SC)	Visit from university librarian: update on library facilities and online searching	
Nov. 00	Preventing school exclusions: theory and practice (YM)	Working with the school community: collaboration considered	Sheila's birthday!
Dec. 00	Integrating inquiry with practice: review of evidence emerging from the group's inquiry work	School cultures workshop	Christmas meal after the session
Jan. 01	Leading learning: reflections on managing a department (SP)	Exploring concepts of leadership	
Feb. 01	Book/article reviews (everyone to choose something relevant to their development work)	Making writing critical workshop	
Mar. 01	What do pupils tell us about their learning in science? (PT)	Analysing qualitative data	Guidance on MA submissions
Apr. 01	Writing reports for the school bulletin (all)	Reviewing the impact of development work	Planning the programme for next term

3 A programme for a support group (example)

Ethical principles for a support group

Groups should draw up their own list of principles after discussion.

1. Discussion that takes place in the group and in individual tutorials must be regarded as absolutely confidential.

2. It is unethical for any individual to make use of disclosures made within the group in other decision-making contexts.

3. Each individual's writing and portfolio should be regarded as their own property and should be used entirely at their own discretion.

4. Full consideration should be given to ethical principles in any inquiry activities, including the need to seek permission before gathering evidence, informing fully those involved, respecting confidentiality, preserving anonymity and protecting the vulnerable.

5. In the writing of evaluative material and the presenting of reports, group members should avoid identifying individual people (colleagues, pupils or others) who might feature in the data, or the school itself, where appropriate.

6. Where individuals can be identified because of the context, the writer should always seek the agreement of those identified, first as to the validity of the data and secondly as to whether the material may be published.

7. Group members have the right to develop a critical analysis of current practices and policies without fear of damage to their standing in the school, but have a responsibility to ensure that this is done purposefully and sensitively.

4 Ethical principles for a support group (example)

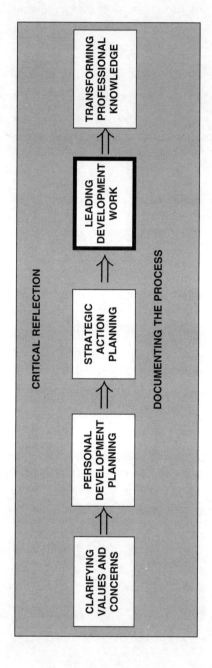

A framework for teacher-led development work

CRITICAL REFLECTION

| CLARIFYING VALUES AND CONCERNS | PERSONAL DEVELOPMENT PLANNING | STRATEGIC ACTION PLANNING | LEADING DEVELOPMENT WORK | TRANSFORMING PROFESSIONAL KNOWLEDGE |

DOCUMENTING THE PROCESS

© David Frost and Judy Durrant 2003

5 A framework for teacher-led development work

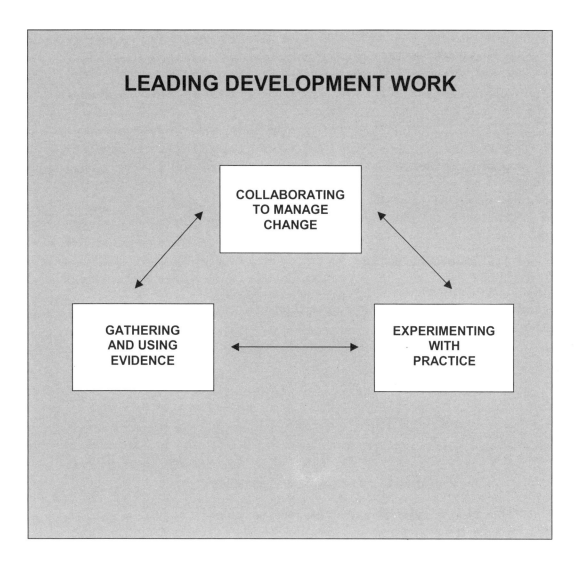

© David Frost and Judy Durrant 2003

6 Leading development work

OUTCOMES

1. Impact on pupils' learning:

- Improved attainment

- Improved disposition

- Improved metacognition

2. Impact on teachers

- Classroom practice

- Personal capacity

- Interpersonal capacity

3. Impact on the school as an organisation

- Structures and processes

- Culture and capacity

4. Impact beyond the school

- Critique and debate

- Creation and transfer of professional knowledge

- Improvements in social capital in the community

© David Frost and Judy Durrant 2003

7 Outcomes of teacher-led development work

Keeping a journal

What to focus on

> development work related to your personal development priorities

> action arising from your action plan

> your professional learning

> impact on your colleagues and the school as an organisation

> the development of your leadership capacity

> issues arising from data gathering

When to make entries

> at a certain time each day or week/after particular events or incidents

> in the flow of your daily work in the classroom, in meetings, around the school

> at times when you can stand back, such as at a conference or on a journey away from school

How to structure your journal

> open-ended, organic, naturalistic

> using frameworks, headings, questions

> by events such as meetings

How to keep the journal

> in a notebook

> on loose-leaf proformas

> on a computer

> on audio tape

8 Keeping a journal

Exploring the issues in classroom practice

Write a short narrative about a recent experience, ideally classroom-based. Where and when did it occur? What happened?

Then in pairs, for each story in turn, discuss and note down:

---

1. Feelings, judgements and thoughts about the experience

---

2. Questions that arise from the narrative

---

3. Issues that could be explored further

---

9 Exploring the issues in classroom practice

A critical incident in classroom practice
'Alice asks a question ...'
by Jon Sparke

Description:

The incident took place at the end of an 'A' level lesson as the students were leaving to take their lunch. Three of the students were slower in leaving than the others and one, Alice, asked the searching question, which while intimately connected with the lesson context was nonetheless unexpected, "What is the difference between socialism and communism?" What struck me as important was both the context of the questioning and the willingness of all three students to then sit back down, listen and discuss my response.

Contextual explanation:

The students are well motivated 'A' level candidates for whom understanding and being able to tell the difference between technical terms is naturally important. They would need to understand and deploy these terms in their exams. Clearly the terms had been used in the lesson and the students had not been clear on the precise meaning and were keen to have this clarified. It is exactly the pedagogic model we always harp on about at consultation evenings as advice to students who are struggling: "They must learn to ask for help when they need it . . ." The student asking for knowledge and understanding from the 'expert' teacher.

Wider meanings:

Why had the student not asked the question within the context of the lesson?
How many other unasked questions remain left at the end of lessons?
How can I collect and make use of such questions?
Was the question important or was it the communication with the teacher that mattered more?

This last question led me further; upon reflection it occurred to me that the students who had remained were the less articulate ones whose voices were less prominent in lessons. They had also been the only students I had yet to ask to do some special preparation for an additional task. This then provoked further enquiry.

Why had I left these students to last? Had this worried them?

Implications for practice:

The importance of valuing all potential student contributions seems to me paramount. Furthermore these students were those for whom 'A' level history is very challenging: the opportunity to focus on their concerns seemed a moment which should not be ignored, above all because their voices are ones I rarely hear.

Clearly the first batch of issues raised suggests that I need to review lessons in order to develop more and perhaps more importantly better opportunities for such valuable questioning. Asking questions within the lesson context at present is clearly not possible for these students. If I could collect some examples of types of 'unasked question' this could provide insight into the learning obstacles that never get addressed, potentially a fantastic diagnostic tool. Some 'A' level students have their learning of concepts or techniques limited by assumptions the teacher makes about their contextual knowledge and understanding.

Finally I looked at the last questions and resolved that I needed to provide more opportunities for this type of work with these students. At present my 'A' level lessons are not sufficiently differentiated to give me time within them to deal with these students' needs.

Source: Skoyles *et al.*, 1998

10 A critical incident in classroom practice

Two narratives

These narratives are based on a teacher's account of leading the introduction of the Internet and web technologies into modern foreign languages in a secondary school with technology status (i.e. with enhanced facilities and training in ICT), working in particular with a Year 10 French class of 26 pupils. Here she considers the issue of the teacher's role in lessons using the web-based resources.

A plain narrative

The role of the teacher in web-based learning

When I introduced the web-based resources, I was free from the normal classroom duties of leading the students from one activity to another, as all the tasks were on screen. Pupils' level of concentration was so high that I found I could spend time with individuals without worrying about whether the rest of the class was on task. Since I had prepared the resources in advance, with clear instructions on screen, the students needed very little guidance, so I was able to devote quality *teaching* time to individuals or small groups of students, going over the particular points which were at the root of the problem they had encountered, such as an aspect of grammar or dictionary usage. I therefore concluded that students do need communication and interaction with their teacher and benefited from the additional individual attention I was giving them.

In this study, the class was using materials that I had researched and prepared, therefore I was still, though indirectly, 'leading' the class. I was also monitoring work and evaluating the outcomes. The difference was that I no longer had to provide oral instructions as frequently as in a traditional lesson. This is quite different from using an Integrated Learning System style software program, where the teacher is not involved in any kind of preparation and is simply there to supervise. I felt that while my role had certainly changed in the sessions, it was clearly not displaced by the use of ICT. Students said that they found the web sessions useful and enjoyable, but they did not think they could completely replace traditional methods, nor did they wish them to. They found the two approaches to be complementary, rather than the new being a suitable substitute for the old.

A critical narrative

The role of the teacher in web-based learning

It is to be expected that, as in this case study, teachers using ICT extensively will find that their role in the class will change, as confirmed by Fox (1997) and Pickering (1995). The fact that students had the facilities to work at their own pace, along with their reliance on each other for help in the first instance, clearly has implications for the role of the teacher. In this case, I was free from the normal classroom duties of leading the students from one activity to another (all the instructions and tasks were on screen), and the level of concentration was so high as to enable me to spend time with individuals without worrying about whether the rest of the class was on task. Whalley (1995) and Selwyn (1998), among others, highlight the changing role of the teacher in such situations, referring to them as a 'guide' or a 'resource'. Such an interpretation of the changing role of the teacher, certainly in the situation experienced in this case study, is misleading and gives undue credit to the teaching ability of the computer. While it is true that my role in these lessons was different during the Internet sessions from that in a normal classroom setting, I was certainly more than simply a 'guide' for the students. Since I had prepared the resources in advance, with clear instructions on screen, the students in fact needed very little guidance. What emerged was that I was able to devote quality *teaching* time to individuals or small groups of students in a way that is difficult to achieve in a normal classroom, going over the particular points which were at the root of the problem they had encountered, such as an aspect of grammar or dictionary usage. Tait (1997) puts forward similar views in a discussion of the use of online materials. Unless the use of ICT is of a 'drill and practice' variety, then it is unrealistic to expect students to learn without opportunities for communication and interaction with the teacher, as highlighted by the socio-cultural theory proposed by McLoughlin and Oliver (1998). One of the main advantages of the model in this study was precisely that it provided opportunities for teaching and assessment at an individual rather than a whole-class level.

Selwyn's (1998) claim that the use of the Internet in this way is at odds with the 'conventional teacher-led ethos' is also to be challenged. In this study, the class was using materials that I had researched and prepared, therefore I was still, though indirectly, 'leading' the class. The difference was that I no longer had to provide oral instructions as frequently as in a traditional lesson. This is quite different from using an Integrated Learning System (ILS) style software program, where the teacher is not involved in any kind of preparation, has no 'ownership' of the lesson, and has little or no role to play during the session apart from a supervisory one. In this case study, the objectives of the lesson and the methods used to achieve them were entirely teacher driven. Furthermore, both the work during the sessions and the outcomes at the end were monitored by me, rather than the computer. Therefore, while my role had certainly changed in these sessions, it remained crucial to the students' learning and was clearly not displaced by the use of ICT. Technology does not replace the teacher, but rather changes the emphasis of their role (Fox 1997). Whereas in industry new technology is introduced to replace old technology, in education new technology is a tool to be used alongside traditional means (Bottino *et al*. 1998). This is a fair reflection of what the students expressed quite emphatically in interview, that useful and enjoyable though they found the web sessions, they did not think web-based learning could completely replace traditional methods, nor did they wish it to. They found the two approaches to be complementary, rather than the new being a suitable substitute for the old.

Adapted from C. Usher (2000) *Exploring the Use of Information and Communications Technology in Modern Foreign Languages: Does the Integration of ICT Enhance Teaching and Learning?* Centre for Education Leadership and School Improvement Occasional Paper No.3, Canterbury: Canterbury Christ Church University College.

References
Bottino, R. M., Forcheri, P. and Molfino, M. T. (1998) 'Technology transfer in schools: from research to innovation'. *British Journal of Educational Technology*, **29**(2).
Fox, M. (1997) The Teacher is Dead! Long Live the Teacher! Implications of the virtual language classroom. *Active Learning 7*. http://www.cti.ac.uk
McLoughlin, C. and Oliver, R. (1998) 'Maximising the language and learning link in computer learning environments'. *British Journal of Educational Technology*, **29**(2).
Pickering, J. (1995) Teaching on the Internet is learning. *Active Learning 2*, July. http://www.cti.ac.uk
Selwyn, N. (1998) The Internet and schools: an uneasy alliance? *Compute-Ed* Vol. 4 http://www.education.uts.edu.au/projects/comped/Vol4/selwyn.html
Tait, B. (1997) Constructive Internet based learning. *Active Learning 7*, http://www.cti.ac.uk
Whalley, W. B. (1995) Teaching and learning on the Internet. *Active Learning 2*, July. http://www.cti.ac.uk

11 Two narratives

How to make writing critical

In attempting to write a critical narrative a writer must first adopt a critical perspective, one that involves standing back from personal experience and assumes a degree of scepticism. The whole point of the exercise is to challenge our own perspective and taken-for-granted understandings. It is this perspective that will determine which issues are allowed to rise to the surface. It is possible to identify a number of steps in the critical process.

1. **Highlight the issues** – reflect on the experience by examining the evidence and allow the most significant issues to bubble to the surface. Reading relevant literature and discussing the events in question with critical friends will help to identify what is contentious, problematic or interesting.

2. **Locate the issues** – identify the previous work and debates to which these issues belong and compare your experience to that of others in similar circumstances.

3. **Apply the explanations or theories** – bring the literature to bear on the issues, introducing the models, typologies, theoretical tools and perspectives which may appear to be potentially useful in explaining the dilemmas and problems associated with the issues you have raised.

4. **Test or criticise explanations** – explore their adequacy for explaining the phenomena or resolving the dilemmas and problems by discovering the flaws in their logic and recognising their ideological bases. Draw upon alternative theoretical perspectives from the literature to critique potential explanatory frameworks.

5. **Explore the fit or match to actual experience** – try out alternative explanations for best fit, comparing theories or explanations and illustrating models with examples from the evidence and experience.

6. **Take up a stance on the issues** – make a choice and justify that choice, identifying the value positions that underpin it, putting forward a clear and robust argument, and recognising the implications for professional action.

7. **Review personal understanding** – identify what you have learned from the analysis both in terms of your particular professional context and more generally about the wider field of inquiry: teaching and learning; curriculum; management of change; school development and so on.

Throughout this process, the evidence in the portfolio and the literature must be referred to in order that a potential reader can evaluate the basis of your analysis.

12 How to make writing critical

Examples of evidence

> an initial statement clarifying values and concerns

> a personal development plan

> action plans

> an interview schedule

> a discussion paper written for a department meeting

> a letter to parents explaining a new assessment system

> a budget for a proposed resources centre

> a memo from the head teacher commenting on an action plan

> email comments from pupils on a new science unit

> an extract from a school inspection report

> selected quotations from a journal

> annotated photographs of pupils on a field trip

© David Frost and Judy Durrant 2003

13 Examples of evidence in a portfolio

Generating documentary evidence

Development work without documentation

A teacher has attended a one-day conference about 'questioning techniques'. Following a conversation with the head teacher, she arranges a meeting with a group of colleagues to discuss the matter. In the meeting, the teachers share their practice and explore the new ideas related verbally by the teacher who attended the conference. The group resolves to experiment with these new ideas and arrange further meetings to discuss the impact of this.

Development work enhanced by documentation

A teacher has attended a one-day conference about 'questioning techniques'. Following a conversation with the head teacher, she arranges a meeting with a group of colleagues to discuss the matter. In preparation for the meeting, the teacher produces a digest of the main ideas gleaned. In the meeting, the teachers share their practice and explore the new ideas related verbally by the teacher who attended the conference. The team leader takes notes that record which of the new techniques seem suitable to be experimented with and the questions or issues surrounding their use. The group resolves to experiment with these new ideas and hold further meetings to discuss the impact of this. The teacher who attended the conference offers to provide a framework which can be used by colleagues to keep a record of their classroom experimentation. This not only enhances the experimentation, but also generates useful evidence about the effects of the techniques. In subsequent meetings, the classroom experiences of the teachers are noted and used to produce a report for other teams in the school. The teacher who introduced the questioning techniques assembles all the documentation in a portfolio to be used for her performance management review and for accreditation purposes. An edited version of the portfolio is added to the school's archive so that subsequent development work can take account of this episode and build on it. This archive would be drawn upon in the event of a school inspection, of course.

14 Generating documentary evidence

Uses of a portfolio

> as a private record of events to aid reflection and planning

> as a tool used within a performance management context

> as a basis for review of progress with a senior colleague, advisor, tutor or other critical friend

> as a summative record of achievement to support an application for a new post

> as a submission for the purposes of accreditation

> as a resource for further dissemination activities

> as part of the institutional archive

© David Frost and Judy Durrant 2003

15 Uses of a portfolio

Principles for portfolio construction

1. Select the evidence

There may be so much documentation arising from a school development initiative that it is inaccessible except to you as the person who led the work. Some of it may be insignificant or repetitive. You therefore need to make a careful selection from the evidence, thinking about the nature and purpose of your portfolio (see Resource 15).

2. Order the evidence

The most obvious way to do this is chronologically so that the reader follows a narrative that spans a period of time. However, it may be appropriate to organise the evidence differently, for example in themes or strands. You may find it useful to draw a diagram or timeline against which you can organise the evidence.

3. Label the evidence

Each item of evidence must be labelled in such a way as to enable it to be easily identified and referenced. It is inappropriate to use page numbers that run throughout as in a dissertation, so you may like to devise some kind of coding system and make a list of contents. Portfolios should not need appendices as the evidence is integrated throughout.

4. Add explanatory commentary

Items of evidence alone will not be intelligible unless they are accompanied by commentary which puts the evidence in context, explains its origin in terms of audience and purpose and provides some rationale for the inclusion of the evidence in the portfolio.

5. Add a critical narrative

This is an analysis and interpretation written in narrative form, telling a 'story' in the first person, drawing on the relevant literature and on the evidence to account for the process of the development work and to engage in a critical discussion about the issues arising. We believe that a critical narrative is essential for the full development of professional understanding, whether or not the portfolio is being submitted for accreditation.

6. Bind the portfolio

The documents presented in the portfolio need to be preserved in order, so it is vital that they are bound together carefully. In our experience, a ring binder is best for keeping the elements in order during portfolio construction, and spiral binding is best once the portfolio is complete. The use of plastic 'pockets' should be avoided; the pages of the portfolio should be immediately accessible and easily turned.

© David Frost and Judy Durrant 2003

16 Principles for portfolio construction

Portfolio review

Work in pairs to talk through your portfolios in turn, or use this sheet for individual review.

1. Evidence
What evidence has been gathered? Has it been processed in any way? In what form(s) will it be presented in the portfolio? Will you have to select, e.g. by choosing examples as illustrations of the wider body of evidence?

Comments   *Action points*

2. Commentary
To what extent will a new reader be able to comprehend the development work represented by the portfolio? Can you make it easier to follow? What labelling and coding system is appropriate? What is the structure of the document as a whole? What additional commentary is needed?

Comments   *Action points*

3. Critical writing
What critical writing has been completed already? What are the other key issues and areas that need to be explored? How will you draw on the evidence and the literature? Have you found an appropriate style and voice?

Comments   *Action points*

4. Professional and academic requirements
To what extent does the portfolio meet the requirements of the school and/or the accrediting body? Has it the right elements, length, format, presentation of text, use and referencing of literature and so on? To what extent have assessment criteria been met?

Comments   *Action points*

Summary of priorities for action

17 Portfolio review

From portfolio to dissertation

Examples of items in the portfolio	Examples of corresponding chapters in the dissertation
Initial statement *Personal development plan* *Notes of meeting with the Head to discuss development priorities*	**Introduction:** Set out the focus of your development work and explore its origins. Write in the first person about your role, responsibilities, professional concerns, values and interests. Account for your undertaking of the development work.
Discussion paper for a working party *First action plan* *Materials produced for*	**Chapter One:** Explore the key concepts relevant to the focus of the development. Examine published accounts of practice and research. Explain and justify the intended action, including the evidence gathering strategies. Explore the strategic issues, obstacles and constraints.
Evidence from an audit of practice *Report on the audit written for senior management team* *Materials produced for a staff meeting to discuss the audit*	**Chapter Two:** Draw on the evidence gathered in the initial audit of practice and related discussions within school, to explore the problems and issues. Give an account of the initial meetings with senior management and staff and explore the strategic issues arising.
Evidence collected for evaluation *An evaluation report* *Notes from conversations with colleagues* *Minutes of meetings*	**Chapter Three:** Tell the story of the development work, e.g. experimenting with an aspect of classroom practice and gathering evidence for an evaluation. Include critical discussion about the evaluation process and the issues arising during the experimentation.
Critical narrative	**Chapter Four:** Write a reflective account of the process of change as a whole. Explore the issues about leading development work.
Extracts from journal *Notes from progress review with senior colleague*	**Chapter Five:** Conclude with reflections on your professional learning and achievement, as a teacher and as a leader of development work.

© David Frost and Judy Durrant 2003

18 From portfolio to dissertation

Clarifying values and concerns

The prompt questions under the headings are merely illustrative. Use these and similar questions to help your partner reflect.

1. Professional history

How long have you been teaching? What posts have you held? How has your role changed over the years? What have you specialised in?

2. Role last year

Who did you teach? What specific responsibilities did you have? Did you take on any additional projects or initiatives on a voluntary basis?

3. Issues arising last year

What were the main obstacles? What emerged as your strengths? What did you struggle with? What did you feel was left unfinished? What would you have done differently?

4. School development priorities

What does the school need to develop this year? What are the priorities and how will they affect you? How are you helping to take these priorities forward?

5. Role this year

What are you responsible for this year? What will your professional learning be focused on? What are the main challenges for you this year?

6. Consultation

Who would you talk to about your role or personal development priorities? Who would you need to consult about any development work you might want to tackle? Who would you go to for support when progress is difficult?

7. Strengths and needs

What strengths are you going to be able to draw upon in carrying out your responsibilities this year? What professional learning will you need to engage in? What kind of support do you think you will need to achieve what lies before you?

8. Values and interests

What are your core professional values? What values underlie your current professional concerns? Is there any mismatch between your personal values and your professional practice or practice more generally?

9. Hopes and aspirations

What would you like to see improved in this school? How do you think you can best contribute to that improvement?

19 Clarifying values and concerns (discussion sheet)

Clarifying values and concerns

1. Professional history

2. Role last year

3. Issues arising last year

4. School development priorities

5. Role this year

6. Consultation

7. Strengths and needs

8. Values and interests

9. Hopes and aspirations

10. Other

20 Clarifying values and concerns (guide sheet)

INITIAL STATEMENT
Clara Peggotty

Professional history

My first degree was in biology and I specialised in science during my PGCE. I have now been teaching for five years. The first two years in Essex I taught Year 5 classes and found these very challenging. I found it hard to think about anything beyond classroom organisation and behaviour management. I made some contribution to science in Year 4 but was very dependent on the deputy head who did most of the planning. In my last post, I was much more confident and was able to use my science knowledge more by teaching lead lessons in Years 4–6 and working with the science coordinator to support my colleagues. This experience convinced me that not only do I need to develop my science work for the sake of my professional satisfaction, but that subject coordination would provide me with the opportunity to develop my management skills.

Since starting at my current school I have necessarily concentrated on my own Year 5/6 class, although I have taught a weekly session for the other Year 5/6 class and had some informal discussions with the teachers of the two Year 3/4 classes.

Current concerns

(a) Teaching approach
From informal contact with the other Year 3/4 classes it seems clear to me that science teaching is far too teacher-driven at the moment. Understandably colleagues who do not have science backgrounds seem to lack confidence, particularly when it comes to the development of investigational skills.

(b) Resources
This is linked to the question of teaching approach: in order to promote investigational skills colleagues need access to resources beyond the textbook we are currently using. More importantly they need the confidence and skills to organise and use those resources in investigational activities.

(c) Professional development
The provision of the primary science course by the LEA is limited because of the expense, particularly that involved in supply cover. It is not practical to send each member of staff on this course. Perhaps we need instead to develop a school-based or cluster-based solution.

The school's development priorities

The development of science is clearly identified as a priority – next year there is a budget of £1500 allocated. However, another priority is 'improving the quality of teaching and learning' and I think that the development of investigational approaches could also fit in with this development work. This will enable us to stretch the funding by pooling resources.

Strengths and needs

I am confident about my own expertise in science teaching and, if it were just a matter of my own practice, I am sure that the situation could be improved rapidly. However, my informal audit of the situation around the school leads me to believe that I am going to find the job of developing science teaching in the way I would be happy with very challenging. I have had no formal training in leadership and management and wonder whether I would have sufficient support in that area.

Values and interests

I am committed to the idea that science depends on the ability to take a sceptical view of things; to be able to suspend your judgement until you have the evidence. In fact I think that these sorts of scientific values make a really important contribution to teaching and learning in general. I am interested as much in the promotion of these values as I am in the bits of specialist knowledge that some colleagues think they need and I have. So I want to avoid being seen as the person who writes list of facts and so on. My role is not just about knowing what has to be taught and writing the scheme of work accordingly. I want to work with my colleagues to try to develop our approach to teaching and learning.

Consultation

I will need to build links with the LEA Advisory Service having had no contact with them in this region so far. I will need a critical friend to explore both the resources that will be needed and also the challenges I will face in leading a review of classroom practice.

21 Initial statement (example) © David Frost and Judy Durrant 2003

Supporting teacher-led development work: key points for head teachers and principals

These have been selected from among 20 points arising from our Impact Project research (Frost and Durrant 2002a). The essential message to head teachers and principals is:

BE THE GUARDIAN OF MAXIMUM LEVERAGE

Pay attention to focus

Some starting points for development are more productive than others. Research can be used to identify the strands of development that have the highest effect size. Head teachers/principals need to assess the energy input against the potential effect size and ensure that teachers do not wear themselves out for little reward (see Hargreaves 2001 for a discussion about leverage).

Pay attention to synergy

In the Impact Project research, teachers saw multiple initiatives as a major problem. Their energy is divided and their attention is diverted and fragmented. It is up to the head teacher/principal who has better knowledge of various plans and priorities, both internal and external, to protect them from conflicts over multiple initiatives; to help them reconcile their personal priorities with school priorities; to interpret and channel external pressures and ensure that once a teacher-led development project has been agreed, it has the same weight as other initiatives.

Pay attention to communication

Development work can be undermined when members of the senior management or leadership team are not all aware of the range of development work going on in the school. Senior managers are well positioned to make the links between strands of development, the combined effect of which is more powerful.

22 Supporting teacher-led development work: key points for head teachers and principals

PERSONAL DEVELOPMENT PLAN

David Copperfield

Role and responsibilities

I am a science teacher in my third year of teaching. I have been contributing to the writing and review of schemes of work and see myself continuing to do so throughout the coming year. However I am also a group tutor for Year 10 and I am interested in developing the pastoral side of my work.

Focus for development

I recently read a journal article about student councils, elected bodies that give students a direct involvement in decision-making in the school. I followed this up by attending a course on citizenship and am now very keen to pursue this idea. It presents an opportunity for students to learn citizenship through active participation, contributing to citizenship within the National Curriculum and to the school aim to 'develop the school as an inclusive community'. I would like to explore the possible development of a student council in my school.

Leading this development is likely to demand management skills I may not have and also I am a relatively junior member of staff. I will therefore need to secure support from the senior management team and talk to the deputy head about strategies for managing the consultation process and the subsequent implementation of the project. I will also need the support of the head of science since this will run alongside my departmental work.

Development priorities

The student council project, if approved, will be very time-consuming, especially in the developmental stage. The process of consultation will probably take from September to December 2002, including presentations to the senior management team, the governing body, the students and the pastoral team. This will be followed by introduction of the council in the following two terms. Review and reporting will happen regularly and recommendations will be made to refine the development in the following year.

While the development work is proceeding, and particularly after the initial consultation process, I will ensure that I maintain my focus on development of the science schemes of work to be introduced from September 2003.

23 Personal development plan (example)

Personal development plan (guide sheet)

Name _____ Date _____

Role and responsibilities

Focus for development

Development priorities

24 Personal development plan (guide sheet)

Planning for impact

> Impact on pupils

> Impact on teachers

> Impact on the school as an organisation

> Impact beyond the school

© David Frost and Judy Durrant 2003

25 Planning for impact

A teacher's development work
What motivates children to learn?

Alison is an English teacher in a secondary school. When she first joined her school's Developing Teaching and Learning group, she reflected on her professional history, concerns and responsibilities in order to determine her personal development priorities. She decided to focus on a difficult class of 12 boys and two girls that she takes for English. The pupils have low ability and a range of special educational needs and behaviour problems.

In discussions with her critical friend from the university, she decided to interview each of the pupils in turn. She asked a colleague to take the class while she interviewed the pupils. She also began some preliminary reading on behaviour, motivation and gender issues. Entering into a serious dialogue about their learning in the interviews seemed to have a positive effect on the pupils.

Alison analysed the interview data and brought her findings to the Developing Teaching and Learning group. She presented them as a series of statements about what helps these pupils to learn. For example:

> These pupils like work in manageable sections with a time limit.
> They respond well to work involving characters with whom they identify.
> It is important to them that the teacher thinks they can do the work.
> The 'can do' or 'can't do' spreads through the class – if some can, it encourages the others.
> Talking to pupils about their learning boosts their self-esteem and perception of themselves as learners.

The members of the group – all colleagues from the same school – revealed some of their own experiences and contributed ideas and suggestions. The meeting included some input from the university tutor on listening to pupils' voices, particularly the work of Rudduck and Flutter (2000) and Fielding (1998). The papers discussed had a revelatory effect on the group. It was exciting to find that work from the 'academic' educational research community supports what is evident in the particular school context. It also provided useful ideas and conceptual frameworks for discussion which led to a better understanding of pupils' perspectives on learning.

The university tutor wrote up the meeting as a series of points arising from the discussion and this was distributed to all members of the group. Alison began to make changes to her practice on the basis of evidence she had gathered, the discussion with colleagues and critical friends and her reading. One of the things she did was to hold an 'awards ceremony' to hand pupils back their low-scoring exam papers, identifying something positive for each one and giving out sweets. She adjusted worksheets to include more visual material, structured tasks and vocabulary prompts, and put pupils' work on the walls in displays built up over time to reinforce the learning. She planned to take the group bowling to reward their progress and to forge even better relationships with them.

Stimulated by Alison's work with these pupils, the coordinator of the Developing Teaching and Learning group led a discussion session on motivation at a network conference. At the request of the group, the university critical friend also began gathering evidence about pupils' perceptions of learning and motivation more widely across the school. Alison and the group coordinator wrote an article for the network journal, setting out the preliminary ideas arising from the inquiry and emphasising the value of listening to pupils. This was published on the network web site and handed out at conferences. It was then discussed in other groups in the network and has encouraged more teachers to enter into dialogue with individual pupils about their learning.

© David Frost and Judy Durrant 2003

26 A case study of a teacher's development work: Alison's story

Planning for impact

1. IMPACT ON PUPILS

a) Improved attainment

> Test or exam results may be improved
> Subject knowledge may be increased and/or skills developed
> Learning in other curriculum areas (e.g. citizenship) may be improved
> *Which pupils will be involved? What aspects of knowledge? What will pupils be able to understand and do better? What evidence will you be looking for?*

b) Improved disposition

> More positive attitudes to school/particular subjects may be fostered
> Motivation to learn may be increased
> Confidence and self-esteem may be increased
> Behaviour may be improved
> *What indices of behaviour and disposition are currently being used? What changes in practice may lead to improvements in disposition? Which pupils may be involved? What evidence will you look for?*

c) Improved metacognition

> Self-awareness may be developed
> Capacity to reflect on and evaluate own learning may be increased
> *What changes in practice might increase pupils' thinking skills and self-awareness? Which pupils might be affected? How might this be evident?*

2. IMPACT ON TEACHERS

a) Improved classroom practice

> You and your colleagues may adopt new practices
> You and your colleagues may improve established practices
> *What changes or amendments to your practice do you envisage? How do you think colleagues may be involved or affected? What evidence will demonstrate that these new practices are more effective?*

b) Improved personal capacity

> You and your colleagues may acquire new skills and strategies
> You and your colleagues may gain knowledge and understanding
> You and your colleagues may develop personal attributes (e.g. emotional intelligence; self-awareness; confidence), greater purpose and commitment
> *What kinds of professional skills and knowledge do you hope to develop yourself? How may colleagues' skills and knowledge increase? How will you determine the extent to which personal capacity has improved?*

c) Improved interpersonal capacity

> You and your colleagues may participate more actively in school development
> You and your colleagues may develop skills in building and maintaining professional relationships
> *In what ways might participation and involvement increase? What kinds of skills are needed to build better relationships for teaching and learning? What evidence will you be looking for?*

3. IMPACT ON THE SCHOOL AS AN ORGANISATION

a) Improved structures and processes

> - There may be more effective decision-making structures and processes
> - Patterns of working may become more collaborative
> - Leadership may become more inclusive and better structured
>
> *What structural changes will you be looking for? What changes in process do you envisage? How will you determine the extent to which teachers are working more collaboratively? What indicators will you use to identify and evaluate changes in leadership?*

b) Improved culture and capacity

> - Collegial relationships and levels of professional discourse may improve
> - Beliefs and values may become more coherent and practice more consistent
> - Use of evidence may become greater and more effective
>
> *How might you influence and analyse the school culture? What will you be looking for in terms of consistency and coherence? How does the school currently use evidence and how might you determine that improvements have been made?*

4. IMPACT BEYOND THE SCHOOL

> - You may share your ideas and good practice with teachers in other schools
> - You may publish accounts of your work through networks, web sites and journals
> - You may contribute to better relationships in the local community
>
> *What contributions might you be able to make? Which contacts, groups and networks might benefit from your work? How will you document your contributions to wider discussion and to the learning of others beyond the school?*

© David Frost and Judy Durrant 2003

27 Planning for impact (guide sheet)

Strategic action planning:
considering the obstacles and opportunities

Note what you know about the following factors. Use the notes when you consult mentors, critical friends and colleagues.

1. Links with other initiatives

How can I maximise synergy in relation to other policies, agendas and initiatives?

2. The micro-political terrain

What is the pattern of interests, values, aspirations and power of the key protagonists in the school? How can I take these into account and work with them?

3. The leadership conditions

How would I assess the structure and quality of leadership in the school and what are the implications for my development work?

4. The provision of external support

How would I assess the structure and quality of external frameworks of support and challenge available to me? Are there advisers or consultants available who could help?

5. The organisational structures and processes

What are the structures and processes for decision-making and communication within the school and how can I work with these to further my development work? What are the key opportunities for exercising leadership?

6. The prevailing organisational culture

What are the dominant values, beliefs and normal practices of colleagues? Are there sub-cultures? Is the culture likely to be supportive of my initiative? How can I work with these cultural factors, and how can I have an impact on them?

© David Frost and Judy Durrant 2003

28 Strategic action planning: considering the obstacles and opportunities

ACTION PLAN
Jacob Marley

Development priority

In order to respond to the Department for Education and Skills Year 9/10 initiative to strengthen careers guidance for young people, it has been agreed that I will undertake to devise and deliver a staff development conference for the Year 9 and 10 tutor teams. The funding allocated through the Careers Service allows for a hotel-based event with an overnight stay.

Consultation

I need to discuss this action plan with Herbert Pocket, the professional development coordinator, Bill Sykes, the PSHE coordinator and Miss Havisham, the advisor at the Careers Service.

Aims of the conference

The tutor team is required to deliver a PSHE programme within which there is time (four hours) for the delivery of careers education and guidance. The scheme of work needs to be devised and materials prepared. There is also a need to facilitate the sense of being a team since these colleagues are not used to collaborating on the PSHE programme and it would be useful to work together on other aspects of the programme in future.

Preparation for the residential

The scheme of work: I intend to organise a review of the lessons that were taught last year by approaching each of the tutors personally for a conversation based on a simple schedule of questions such as: How useful were the materials? What problems did you experience with the student activities? I will also visit the current Year 10 classes during their PSHE lessons for a brief group discussion about their experience of careers guidance this year and their suggestions on what they would find useful. I shall summarise the issues arising and present this summary at the beginning of the residential. The discussion should lead us to some clear ideas for planning the new scheme.

The team building: I intend to read about team building (the chapter in Everard and Morris looks useful) and analyse the present team membership using a team analysis exercise (probably the Belbin categories set out in Everard and Morris). I shall draw up a brief paper setting out the key issues about the operation of teams. I may decide to put this list of issues on the table at the start of the residential as a way of helping us think about how to work together more effectively.

Evaluation

I shall record, in my journal, critical incidents that occur during the residential in order to be able to reflect afterwards on how well we dealt with the team issues. I shall also ask for feedback from the tutors at the end of the residential.

Outcomes

Following the residential I shall type up the agreed scheme of work and present it to the PSHE coordinator and the careers advisers for feedback.

The original list of team issues, my journal entries and the feedback from tutors and pupils will enable me to produce an evaluation report which will be presented to our school's staff development coordinator and the Careers Service advisor. These two outcomes will be complete by the end of November.

Possible follow-up

I will discuss with the tutor team the possibility of evaluating the new scheme of work in action.

Evidence for the portfolio

This will include this action plan, the summary of team issues, the summary of issues about the previous scheme of work, the summary of pupils' comments, the new scheme of work itself, the evaluation report and supporting evidence.

29 Action plan (example)

Sample development priorities

Development priority A

Estella, a head of sixth form, has been allocated funding to improve the environment and ethos in the sixth form. Staff have raised concerns about the lack of motivation to study, lack of study skills and underachievement within the sixth form.

Context: The sixth form currently occupies a shabby building on the edge of the school grounds. The 'common room' has old furniture donated by parents. There are some tables at one end where students may work. The room has been decorated by students with murals depicting cartoon characters. Staff and parents have commented on the untidy appearance of students. When not in lessons, they are often seen playing football, chatting and listening to music.

Development priority B

Pip, a science teacher, has agreed to review and develop the science curriculum at Key Stage 3 in order to make best use of information technology.

Context: Pip is in his third year of teaching. He is very enthusiastic and has particular interest and skills in IT. A room adjoining the science area has recently been fitted out with computers with Internet facilities but this is currently underused. All the school staff have received compulsory IT training; those teaching Key Stage 3 science have varying experience and confidence and two have not used computers in their classroom since the training last year.

Development priority C

Following some worrying comments arising from a school inspection, Tim, a teacher of Year 6 (10–11-year-olds) at a large urban primary school, has agreed to prioritise the development of his own teaching style.

Context: He currently feels dissatisfied with the quality of students' learning, with the standard of students' behaviour and engagement with the tasks set. He has considerable experience but feels he has neglected his pedagogy because of all the paperwork associated with recent educational reforms. His head teacher is supportive and they have a good relationship.

30 Sample development priorities

Action plan (guide sheet)

Focus for development
The development priority or aspect of it, the context

Proposals for change
New practice, implementation, classroom experiment, the hoped-for outcomes

Collaboration and consultation, reporting
What, with whom, when?

Evidence-gathering strategies
Questions/issues, data needed, instruments and techniques

Targets and timescales
What and by when?

Evaluation and review
With whom, when?

Outcomes/impact
In relation to development priorities

31 Action plan (guide sheet)

127

Dimensions of
the role of the change agent

> **personal vision-building**

> **inquiry**

> **mastery**

> **collaboration**

(Source: Fullan 1993)

32 Role of the change agent

Leadership tasks		
Coordinate the activities of individuals	Bid for required resources	Provide clear leadership
Make contacts with outside agencies and other schools	Stimulate discussion on key issues	Define the objectives clearly
Organise regular and effective meetings	Provide links to useful sources of expertise	Provide a forum for discussion and debate
Help colleagues to analyse current practice	Explain new ideas to colleagues in a rational and persuasive way	Clarify the issues for colleagues
Be exemplary	Facilitate the growth of trust between colleagues	Give colleagues clear indications of weaknesses in their current practices
Give colleagues clear indications of ways in which their practice could be improved	Help colleagues to identify their strengths	Facilitate self-evaluation
Encourage better working relationships between team members	Provide anxious colleagues with reassurance	Share your own strengths and weaknesses
Evaluate colleagues' progress	Bid for time to devote to team deliberations	Organise and lead staff development activities
Promote colleagues' confidence and self-esteem	Give colleagues praise and recognition for any positive development	Provide information about new ideas and developments

33 Leadership tasks (labels for cards)

Descriptions of school cultures

The individualistic culture

> working in isolation
> protection from feedback through etiquette of privacy
> feedback restricted to own classes
> limited motivation to improve performance
> low levels of discussion with colleagues
> poor environment for professional learning
> playing it safe, no risks, conservative approach
> help not sought or welcomed
> high expectations and guilt

The Balkanised culture

> teachers develop loyalty to separate groups
> high levels of competition between groups
> departments behave like independent city states
> groups develop their own dominant pedagogic codes/styles
> poor communication between groups
> tendency to assume negative stereotypes about members of other groups
> frequent conflicts over time, space and other resources
> defence of territory becomes a predominant concern of group
> tendency to oppose any whole-school initiatives

The collaborative culture

> team teaching and joint planning are features
> continuous self-renewal is taken for granted as a fact of life
> ongoing professional learning is evident
> joint work such as action research, mutual observation
> collaborative projects are evident
> high levels of trust and openness
> banter, gestures, jokes and celebrations reflect mutual understanding and sympathy
> failure and uncertainty are discussed rather than hidden from view
> examination of values and purposes is a continuous process
> teachers' voices are strong and so disagreements are visible
> colleagues are recognised as persons
> colleagues are empowered

(Source: Fullan and Hargreaves 1992)

34 Descriptions of school cultures

Engaging with the school as an organisation

What advice would you give these teachers? What strategies do you recommend?

Incident of engagement A

Nancy, a teacher newly appointed to a post with responsibility for literacy, has concerns about the amount of support pupils initially receive on entering high school from a variety of backgrounds. The school is in a densely populated urban district with a high proportion of pupils from low-income families, many of whom have English as a second language.

Teachers are working hard and while fully committed, they are reluctant to take on any additional work. They have recently been demoralised by the school's poor inspection report which highlights literacy as a major concern, requiring that it is a priority in the school improvement plan. Nancy has voiced her concerns to the principal who is generally sympathetic but who wants to concentrate on behaviour and motivation issues with older age groups where test results show greater levels of underachievement. There is a small amount of external support available through the district but this is threatened by budget cuts.

Nancy is convinced that with better and more directed and individualised support in the first year at the school, pupils will develop more self-confidence and better study skills and their literacy will improve, leading to improved standards across the school.

Incident of engagement B

Oliver is the chair of a working party that has been conducting systematic inquiry into pupils' experience of bullying. There is evidence that the school has a serious problem.

He is not sure whether to go straight to the governors (school board) or to ask to attend the senior management team meeting to make a presentation. In the past the head teacher has dealt severely with bullying and has presented a policy of 'zero tolerance'. However, the investigations suggest that much bullying is not formally reported. One member of the working party is also responsible for marketing the school and there is a lot of local competition in the recruitment of new students. He warns that the school has falling numbers and must present a positive image otherwise staffing will be cut.

35 Engaging with the school as an organisation

Using evidence

1. To identify or clarify a problem

What is the problem and what is its extent? What is likely to be the best course of action?

2. To examine alternative practice

What do observation and accounts of others' practice tell us about our own?

3. To monitor and evaluate classroom practice

How effective are our teaching strategies in helping pupils to learn?

4. To validate proposals for change

What are the potential benefits of change?

5. To adapt a new practice to fit our situation

How are ideas from elsewhere fitting into the unique characteristics of our own classroom or school and how might they need to be modified?

6. To give voice to colleagues, students, parents and other stakeholders

How can evidence from different perspectives be used to shape policy and practice?

7. To monitor the process of development

What can individuals and our organisation learn about leading and managing change?

36 Some powerful evidence situations

Strategies for integrating evidence gathering with everyday practice

1. **Use evidence that is already available**

   (e.g. test scores, minutes of meetings, professional development portfolios, pupils' work . . .)

2. **Use creative strategies for collecting evidence**

   (e.g. group interviews with pupils, discussion groups of staff with a spokesperson to report back, a videotape of a lesson, emailed comments from pupils at the end of their homework . . .)

3. **Investigate a range of techniques**

   (besides the ubiquitous questionnaire and individual interview, through selected reading about teacher research and action research)

4. **Plan time to discuss the evidence with colleagues**

   (request time during existing meetings, bid for a slot on a development day, etc.)

5. **Keep a journal**

   (collect ideas and reflections on the inquiry process as you proceed, using, for example, a tape recorder in the car, notes in the margin of your planner . . .)

6. **Get practical help**

   (a university research student? an adviser from the LEA or school district? a parent? a governor?)

37 Strategies for integrating evidence gathering with everyday practice

Practical inquiry to support development work

1. Evidence-gathering methods should be 'fit for purpose'

What evidence do you need in order to assess the current situation and to evaluate change?

How are you going to collect that evidence?

How can you tailor it to your purpose by piloting strategies and instruments?

How are you going to use the evidence to support your leadership of change?

2. Evidence-gathering strategies should be efficient and institution-friendly

Have you recognised and made full use of data that already exists?

How do your plans for data gathering avoid disrupting teaching and integrate with your own and others' practice?

Can you borrow and adapt devices designed and used by others?

Have you chosen straightforward strategies that others can use?

Have you chosen strategies that produce a type and amount of data that you have time to analyse?

How have you taken account of ethical issues and allowed for possible conflict and dissent?

3. Inquiry should be part of a managed change process

Have you drawn colleagues and others into the inquiry activity?

Have you planned time for analysis, interpretation and validation of data?

Have you planned to engage with the school as an organisation – reporting, consulting, collaborating, debating, influencing, policy-making?

Have you bid for sufficient resources for appropriate staff development activities?

Have you chosen inquiry strategies that raise awareness, encourage debate, maximise involvement?

Are you gathering data about the management of change itself to maximise personal and organisational learning?

Reflecting on the outcomes of your development work

This guide sheet can be used at any stage of the development process. Consider the four kinds of outcomes and use the bullet points to prompt your thinking.

1. Outcomes for pupils
> increase in attainment and/or knowledge and in subjects/wider curriculum
> improvements in motivation, attitudes and behaviour
> increased self-confidence and self-esteem
> increased self-awareness, understanding, responsibility for own learning
> increased capacity to learn and evaluate own learning

2. Outcomes for your practice and your colleagues' practice
> adoption of new practices or improvements in existing practices
> improvement in pedagogical knowledge and skills and wider professional knowledge
> increased self-awareness, confidence, commitment
> clarification of purpose
> increased participation, involvement and collaborative working
> improved professional relationships

3. Outcomes for the school as an organisation
> improved structures for communication and decision-making
> improved leadership structures and increased shared leadership
> more collaborative working and better collegial relationships
> better use of evidence to underpin practice
> better quality of professional discourse
> more consistency of practice and coherence of values and beliefs

4. Outcomes beyond the school
> publication of accounts of development work through conferences, web sites, journals
> contributions to policy formation or debate
> collaborations with teachers in other schools
> improved relationships with the local community

© David Frost and Judy Durrant 2003

39 Reflecting on the outcomes of your development work

Reflecting on outcomes

Description of outcomes

Evidence available

Implications for future development

40 Reflecting on outcomes

Reflecting on outcomes: Julie's story

Julie attended a course about learning styles two years ago and decided to try to introduce a greater variety of learning styles into her teaching because she believed that it would motivate and engage pupils, and lead to higher attainment. She spent some time searching for additional reading and information on learning styles. She used a published questionnaire to determine pupils' preferred learning styles, finding that many pupils preferred kinaesthetic learning and felt that it was more effective. She discussed the results with them to raise awareness of themselves as learners. In the first year she concentrated on developing one unit of work, introducing more variety of learning activities. Evaluations showed that pupils responded well to this, enjoying the lessons more and producing some good quality work which compared favourably with the previous class using the old schemes of work.

In the second year her confidence increased, and she began to approach all her lesson planning with the intention of introducing a wider variety of teaching and learning strategies. She says:

> *I started to make changes to the way I was approaching my teaching: I put up displays, hung words from the ceiling . . . I started to focus on learning objectives with all my classes, changed the way I go about marking books . . . I'm bringing in a lot more different types of learning styles . . . perhaps being a bit more adventurous with some of the groups . . . they are starting to suggest things that'll help them to learn – they say try it this way, because we have talked about how they learn best and they know that's what we're aiming for. It's completely changed the way I look at the kids, the way I look at their learning . . .*

She believes that pupils' attainment has improved, although it is very difficult to determine cause and effect. In her judgement the standard of pupils' work has improved and test results are encouraging.

© David Frost and Judy Durrant 2003

41 Reflecting on outcomes: Julie's story

A case of knowledge transformation: Richard's story

Richard was interested in the potential of work on the 'student voice' to contribute to improvements in teaching and learning in the school where he was an experienced teacher and coordinator of teaching and learning. With the help of two colleagues, he set up an experimental project which involved inviting groups of students to collaborate with them in order to evaluate their teaching. The students were given some basic training in lesson observation techniques and were then asked to generate data that addressed the question: 'What did the teacher do to help you learn?' Richard collected these data and presented them to his colleagues for discussion. This led to a robust evaluation of their teaching approaches. Both Richard and his colleagues noted improvements in their students' commitment to their own learning as well as improvements in their own teaching.

Accounts of this work were shared with the whole staff during one of their regular development days. Colleagues were invited to use the strategies and materials that Richard and his collaborators had developed through this experiment. In his critical narrative, Richard noted the way the work appeared to have contributed to the development of the organisational culture. Colleagues had become more accustomed to discussing teaching and learning in general and the students' perspective in particular. When difficulties with a particular year group arose, it seemed obvious to seek the students' views through a survey and through discussion activities in PSHE lessons. The student voice idea had become embedded in the culture.

Having successfully submitted accounts of his work for the Masters degree programme, Richard concentrated on other dissemination activities. He took up the chair of the LEA sponsored Thematic Research Group on Student Voice and published a brief account of his work on its web page. At the same time he began drafting a chapter for a book about teaching and learning. The publication of his account on the web led to invitations to contribute to programmes of support for other schools. For example, he was asked to lead a seminar about 'student voice' within a leadership development programme funded under the Networked Learning Communities scheme. Richard has now been seconded to the LEA to work as a teaching and learning consultant across the county.

© David Frost and Judy Durrant 2003

42 A case of knowledge transformation: Richard's story

References

Altrichter, H., Posch, P. and Somekh, B. (1993) *Teachers Investigate Their Work: An Introduction to the Methods of Action Research*. London: Routledge.

Angus, L. (1993) 'New leadership and the possibility of educational reform', in Smyth, J. (ed.) *A Socially Critical View of the Self-managing School*. London: Falmer Press.

Argyris, C. and Schon, D. (1996) *Organizational Learning II*. Reading, MA: Addison-Wesley.

Ball, S. J. (1987) *The Micro-politics of the School: Towards a Theory of School Organisation*. London: Methuen.

Bascia, N. and Hargreaves, A. (eds) (2000) *The Sharp Edge of Educational Change: Teaching, Leading and the Realities of Reform*. London: Routledge Falmer.

Bruner, J. (1996) *The Culture of Education*. Cambridge, MA: Harvard University Press.

Crowther, F., Kaagan, S., Ferguson, M. and Hann, L. (2002) *Developing Teacher Leaders: How Teacher Leadership Enhances School Success*. Thousand Oaks, CA: Corwin Press.

Elliott, J. (1998) *The Curriculum Experiment: Meeting the Challenge of Social Change*. Buckingham: Open University Press.

Elliott, J., MacLure, M. and Sarland, C. (1996) *Teachers As Researchers in the Context of Award Bearing Courses and Research Degrees*, a report. Norwich: Centre for Applied Research in Education.

Evans, L. (1998) *Teacher Morale, Job Satisfaction and Motivation*. London: Paul Chapman Publishing.

Fielding, M. (1998) 'Students as researchers: from data source to significant voice', contribution to the symposium *Making a Difference: Taking Seriously the Students' Agenda for School Improvement*. International Congress for School Effectiveness and Improvement (ICSEI), University of Manchester, January 1998.

Frost, D. (1995) 'Reflective action planning: a model for continuing professional development', in Frost, D., Edwards, A. and Reynolds, H. (eds) *Careers Education and Guidance*. London: Kogan Page.

Frost, D. (1997) *Reflective Action Planning for Teachers: A Guide to Teacher-led School and Professional Development*. London: David Fulton Publishers.

Frost, D. (1999) *Teacher-led School Improvement: The Development Through Action Research of a School-based, Award-bearing Form of Support*. Unpublished PhD thesis, Centre for Applied Research in Education, University of East Anglia.

Frost D. (2000) 'Teacher-led school improvement: agency and strategy'. *Management in Education* **14**(4), 21–4 and **14**(5), 17–20.

Frost, D. and Durrant, J. (2002a) 'Teacher-led development work: implications for leadership' (a paper within the 'Leadership for Learning: the Cambridge network' symposium). 15th International Congress for School Effectiveness and Improvement (ICSEI), Copenhagen, 3–6 January 2002.

Frost, D. and Durrant, J. (2002b) 'Teachers as leaders: exploring the impact of teacher-led development work'. *School Leadership and Management*, **22**(2).

Frost, D., Durrant, J., Head, M. and Holden, G. (2000) *Teacher-led School Improvement*. London: Routledge Falmer.

Fullan, M. (1993) *Change Forces: Probing the Depths of Educational Reform*. London: Falmer Press.

139

Fullan, M. (1999) *Change Forces: The Sequel*. London: Falmer Press.

Fullan, M. (2001) *Leading in a Culture of Change*. San Francisco, CA: Jossey-Bass.

Fullan, M. and Hargreaves, A. (1992) *What's Worth Fighting for In Your School? Working Together for Improvement*. Buckingham: Open University Press.

Galton, M. and MacBeath, J. (with Page, C. and Steward, S.) (2002) *A Life in Teaching? Teachers' Working Lives*. London: National Union of Teachers.

Giddens, A. (1984) *The Constitution of Society*. Cambridge: Polity Press.

Gray, J., Hopkins, D., Reynolds, D., Wilcox, B., Farrell, S. and Jesson, D. (1999) *Improving Schools: Performance and Potential*. Buckingham: Open University Press.

Hargreaves, A. (1994) *Changing Teachers, Changing Times: Teachers' Work and Culture in the Postmodern Age*. London: Cassell.

Hargreaves, A., Earl, L., Moore, S. and Manning, S. (2001) *Learning to Change: Teaching Beyond Subjects and Standards*. San Francisco, CA: Jossey-Bass.

Hargreaves, D. (1995) 'School effectiveness, school change and school improvement: the relevance of the concept of culture'. *School Effectiveness and Improvement* 6(1), 23–46.

Hargreaves, D. (1996) *Teaching as an Evidence Based Profession: The TTA Annual Lecture*. London: Teacher Training Agency (TTA).

Hargreaves, D. (1998) 'A new partnership of stakeholders and a national strategy for research in education', in Rudduck, J. and McIntyre, D. (eds) *Challenges for Educational Research: New BERA Dialogues*. London: Paul Chapman Publishing.

Hargreaves, D. (1999a) 'The knowledge-creating school', *British Journal of Educational Studies*, 47(2), 122–44.

Hargreaves, D. (1999b) 'Helping practitioners explore their school's culture', in Prosser, J. (ed.) *School Culture*. London: Paul Chapman Publishing.

Hargreaves, D. (2001) 'A capital theory of school effectiveness and improvement'. *British Educational Research Journal*, 27(4), 487–503.

Harris, A. and Muijs, D. (2002) *Teacher Leadership: A Review of Research*. Nottingham: National College for School Leadership.

Holden, G. (2002a) 'Towards a learning community: the role of mentoring in teacher-led school improvement'. *Journal of In-service Education*, 28(1), 9–21.

Holden, G. (2002b) *Changing Stories: The Impact of Teacher-led Development Work on Teacher, School and Student Learning*. Unpublished PhD thesis, Canterbury: Canterbury Christ Church University College/University of Kent at Canterbury.

Horne, M. (2001) *Classroom Assistance: Why Teachers Must Transform Teaching*. London: Demos.

Johnson, M. and Hallgarten, J. (2002) *From Victims of Change to Agents of Change: The Future of the Teaching Profession*. London: Institute of Public Policy Research.

Lave, J. and Wenger, E. (1991) *Situated Learning: Legitimate Peripheral Participation*. Cambridge: Cambridge University Press.

Leithwood, K. and Jantzi, D. (1990) 'Transformational leadership: how principals can help reform school cultures'. *School Effectiveness and School Improvement* 1(4), 249–80.

MacBeath, J. (1998) 'I didn't know he was ill: the role and value of the critical friend', in Stoll, L. and Myers, K. (eds) *No Quick Fixes: Perspectives on Schools in Difficulty*. London: Falmer Press.

MacBeath, J. (1999) *Schools Must Speak for Themselves: The Case for School Self-evaluation*. London: Routledge.

MacBeath, J. (forthcoming) 'Democratic learning and school effectiveness: Are they by any chance related?', in Moos, L. and MacBeath, J. (eds), *Democratic Learning and School Effectiveness*. London: Paul Chapman.

MacBeath, J. and McGlynn, A. (2002) *Self-evaluation: What's in it for Schools?* London: Routledge Falmer.

MacBeath, J., Schratz, M., Meuret, D. and Jakobsen, L. (2000) *Self-evaluation in European Schools: A Story of Change*. London: Routledge/Falmer.

McLaughlin, M. (1997) 'Rebuilding teacher professionalism in the United States', in Hargreaves, A. and Evans, R. (eds) *Beyond Educational Reform: Bringing Teachers Back In*. Buckingham: Open University Press.

Mitchell, C. and Sackney, L. (2000) *Profound Improvement: Building Capacity for a Learning Community*. Lisse, The Netherlands: Swets and Zeitlinger.

Price Waterhouse Cooper (2001) *Teacher Workload Study: A Report of the Review Commissioned by DfES*. London: Price Waterhouse Cooper.

Rudduck, J. and Flutter, J. (2000) 'Pupil participation and pupil perspective: carving a new order of experience'. *Cambridge Journal of Education*, 30(1), 75–89.

Sammons, P., Hillman, J. and Mortimore, P. (1995) *Key Characteristics of Effective Schools: A Review of School Effectiveness Research* (a report by the Institute of Education for the Office of Standards in Education). London: Institute of Education.

Schon, D. (1983) *The Reflective Practitioner: How Professionals Think in Action*. London: Temple Smith.

Senge, P. (1990) *The Fifth Discipline: The Art and Practice of the Learning Organisation*. New York: Doubleday.

Sergiovanni, T. (2001) *Leadership: What's in it for Schools?* London: Routledge/Falmer.

Skoyles, P. and Sparke, J. (with Durrant, J.) (1998) 'Analysis of critical incidents: testing a framework for developing professional judgement and improving practice through reflection'. *The Enquirer*, Summer 1998.

Stacey, R. (1996a) *Strategic Management and Organisational Dynamics* (2nd edn). London: Pitman.

Stacey, R. (1996b) *Complexity and Creativity in Organisations*. San Francisco, CA: Berrett-Koehler.

Stenhouse, L. (1975) *An Introduction to Curriculum Research and Development*. London: Heinemann.

Stoll, L., MacBeath, J., Smith, I. and Robertson, P. (2001) 'The change equation: capacity for improvement', in MacBeath, J. and Mortimore, P. (eds) *Improving School Effectiveness*. Buckingham: Open University Press.

Times Educational Supplement (1999a) 'Head of year wins £47,000', 21 October.

Times Educational Supplement (1999b) 'The downward spiral of stress', 12 November.

Times Educational Supplement (2000) 'Record payout for school stress', 12 May.

Tripp, D. (1993) *Critical Incidents in Teaching: Developing Professional Judgement*. London: Routledge.

Webb, R. and Vulliamy, G. (1996) 'Impact of ERA on primary management'. *British Educational Research Journal*, 22, 441–58.

Wenger, E. (1998) *Communities of Practice: Learning, Meaning and Identity*. Cambridge: Cambridge University Press.

White, S. K. (1988) *The Recent Work of Jurgen Habermas: Reason, Justice and Modernity*. Cambridge: Cambridge University Press.

Web sites

Best Practice Research Scholarships: http://www.teachernet.gov.uk/
CANTARNET http://education-resources.cant.ac.uk/cantarnet/
National College for School Leadership (2002) *Networked Learning Communities* http://www.ncsl.org.uk/

Index

Resources in Part G are not indexed; they are referenced in the text and listed on p.93.

academic
  publication 50
  requirements 15, 54, 56–7, 59–60, 67, 75
  staff 8, 10
  tutoring 6, 16, 33, 47, 63
accommodation 11
accountability vii, 5–7, 15
accreditation 4, 9–10, 15–16, 20–2, 24, 30, 32, 44–5, 55, 60, 66–7
action
  planning xii, 25, 32, 36–9, 44, 59–61, 81–2
  professional xi, 60
  strategic 1, 5, 25, 59, 62, 81–2
action research 4, 11
administrative arrangements 52
agency *see* teacher agency
agent *see* change, agent
Angus, L. 3
archive 24, 31–2, 55
assignments 9–10, 54, 57
audience 26, 30–1, 49, 66-7, 90
authority 5

Beacon Schools 42
beliefs 26, 28–9, 39, 42
Best Practice Research Scholarships 66
Bruner, J. 3

capacity 3, 58
  building 2, 6–7, 18, 51, 61–2, 65
  interpersonal 1, 4, 53
  leadership xi, 1
  organisational 1, 18, 47, 50, 53, 57
  personal 1, 4, 18, 26–7, 53
case study xii, 7, 20–2, 49, 57, 64
change
  agent xi, 4, 39, 44, 83
  school xi–xii, 1, 25, 56–7
  management of 24–6, 40–4, 60–3, 83–4
  resistance to 1
code of practice 13, 63
collaboration 6, 20, 25, 40–2, 85, 87
collaborative
  arrangements xi, 42
  working xii, 1, 26, 36, 48–50, 53, 55, 64–5, 86
commitment 1, 12, 25, 52
community
  of practice 6–7
  professional 6–7, 25, 48
  school 53
complexity 2, 24, 27, 53, 55

conference 12, 14, 20, 67
consultation 12, 24–8, 31–41, 49–50, 56–8, 87
context 10, 20, 25, 30, 61, 65
coordinator 12, 19
creativity vii
critical
  debate/discourse 5–6, 13, 72–3
  friendship vii, 5–6, 15–16, 24, 28, 33–6, 47, 51–67
  narrative 29–30, 32, 48–9, 54–5, 65
  reflection xii, 16, 19, 24, 27–30, 53–4, 72–3
culture xi, 2, 26, 35, 40, 52, 60, 64, 66, 85–7

data
  analysis 16, 28, 53
  gathering 20, 26, 37, 41, 43–8
  presenting 42
development
  focus 37, 41, 43
  plan, personal 34, 57–9, 77–8
  planning, personal 5, 25, 56–9, 77–8
  priorities
    negotiation of 24–5, 34, 58, 78
    personal 5, 10, 24, 34, 40, 77–8
    pursuing 36, 38
    school xii, 3, 57
dialogue 3, 43, 58
discourse 3, 5–6, 48, 62
discussion 6, 11–12, 26–8, 53–4, 63–4
documenting 24, 30–2, 36, 39, 45, 54–5, 65

educational reform vii, 1, 3
ethical
  issues 13, 47, 55, 87
  principles 19, 63, 71
evaluation xii, 16, 18–20, 26, 35–6, 41–5, 55
evidence
  gathering 19–20, 24, 26, 31, 44–8, 55, 60
  portfolio of 31–2, 61
  types of 32
  use of xii, 15, 26, 29, 31, 44–8, 60, 64–5
experience 5, 7, 18, 24, 26, 29–30, 52–3, 60
experimenting with practice 20, 26, 31, 37, 42–4, 64, 66
expertise 5, 7, 48

framework
  accreditation 9–10
  supporting xi, 4–5, 10, 19, 23–7, 51–2, 69–71
Fullan, M. 2–3, 62, 76, 83
funding 5, 9, 11–12, 14, 18, 67

Giddens, A. 56, 85

Hargreaves, A. 65, 85
Hargreaves, D. 5, 59, 64, 65, 86
head teachers xi, 1–5, 9, 18, 52, 58, 66

impact 9, 18, 20, 26, 34, 36, 40, 47–9, 58, 60, 64–5, 79–80, 90–1
induction 10, 51
initial statement 32, 34, 57
initiatives *see* change; educational reform
inquiry 5–6, 22, 26, 29, 37, 40, 44–8, 59–60, 64–5, 88–9
inspection 17, 26, 31

journal 28–9, 53

knowledge
    creation and transfer vii, 4–7, 20, 26, 48–50, 64–7
    professional *see* professional knowledge

leadership vii, xii, 2, 4, 9, 39, 52, 59
    of development work 25–6, 39–48, 61–4, 83–4
    styles and models of 2–3, 62
    teacher *see* teacher leadership
    team 1, 9
learning
    community 2
    effectiveness xi, 1
    leadership for 4
    organisational xii, 2, 24, 26, 32, 54–5, 58, 65, 90
    professional 2, 7, 13, 24, 28–30, 42, 48–9, 57, 64–6, 90
    pupil 2, 4, 22, 24, 26, 42, 47, 58, 67
library 12, 17, 52
local education authority 7–8, 11, 14, 18, 21–2, 91

MacBeath, J. vii–viii, 3
memorandum of agreement 8, 19
mentoring 44, 50, 51
methodology 5, 28
micro-politics 2, 5–6, 54, 63
Mitchell, C. 2, 85

narrative *see* critical narrative
National College for School Leadership 12, 14
Networked Learning Communities 12, 42, 66
networks xii, 5–7, 13–17, 19–22, 26, 50, 65–7

online activity 19–22, 28, 49
organisational
    capacity *see* capacity, organisational
    conditions 1–2, 5, 35, 85
    culture 4, 8
outcomes 18, 20, 30, 34, 39, 44, 47–50, 59

partnerships xi, 5, 7, 20, 52, 66
performance management 15, 21, 24, 32–3
planning 5, 10, 12, 20, 24, 28, 41, 43, 79
    action *see* action planning
policy vii, 6, 18, 50
portfolio 15, 31–2, 34, 36, 39, 53–7, 59, 61, 66–7, 74–5, 90
power 1–5, 9, 56
practice
    consistency of 1, 3
    professional 2, 44, 48, 64, 66
    sharing good vii, 13, 31, 40, 42

professional
    development vii, xii, 11, 18, 32, 36, 42, 49
    development centre 10–11
    discourse xii
    knowledge xii, 1, 4, 17–18, 26, 44, 54–5
        transformation of *see* knowledge transformation
    programme 12, 51–2, 63
publishing 17–18, 50, 66–7
pupil
    learning *see* learning, pupil
    voice 41–2

reading 16, 28, 30, 45–6, 53, 82, 89
reconnaissance viii, 37, 60
reflection 5–6, 10, 24–8, 33–4, 56, 62–4
    critical *see* critical reflection
reliability 46
reporting 25, 28, 48–50
research 5, 8, 17, 22, 26, 46, 50, 59, 60
review 8–9, 24–5, 60, 75–5
risk-taking 42–3

Sackney, L. 2, 85
school
    effectiveness 1–3
    improvement xi, 1–2, 7, 9, 15–16, 34, 56, 58, 61, 65
Senge, P. 3
Stenhouse, L. 5
strategic thinking 25, 50, 60, 88
strategy 2, 8
support group 5, 9, 11, 13, 19–22, 28, 33, 63–4, 69

teacher
    agency 3–4, 6, 56, 70
    autonomy 1
    leadership vii–viii, xi, 1–7, 52, 61–2, 70–1
    morale 3, 50
    professionalism vii, xi
    recruitment and retention 3
    stress vii, 3
teams 41, 43
technology 14
theory vii
triangulation 46
tutoring *see* academic tutoring

university 5, 7–11, 14, 21, 59, 91
    award-bearing programmes *see* accreditation
    tutor 22, 63, 66

validity 46
values 7, 39
    clarifying 5, 24–5, 28, 33–4, 54, 56–7, 76
    coherence of 1, 3, 67
    of higher education 5
    shared 6, 16
    teachers' 2, 42, 62
valuing teachers 12
vision 2–3, 25, 56
voice
    pupil 41–2
    teacher 18, 26, 29, 48, 50, 57, 66

working party 41
writing 24, 29–30, 34–8, 49–50, 53–7, 66, 72